FIRE IN THE BRAND

An Introduction to the Creative Work and Theology of John Wesley

Howard Alexander Slaatte, Ph.D.

Foreword by Bishop Paul V. Galloway

UNIVERSITY
PRESS OF
AMERICA

LANHAM • NEW YORK • LONDON

Copyright © 1983 by

University Press of America,™ Inc.

4720 Boston Way
Lanham, MD 20706

3 Henrietta Street
London WC 2E 8LU England

Copyright © 1963 by
Howard Alexander Slaatte

Library of Congress Cataloging in Publication Data

Slaatte, Howard Alexander.
    Fire in the brand.

    Reprint. Originally published: New York : Exposition
Press, 1963. (An Exposition-university book)
    Bibliography: p.
    1. Wesley, John, 1703–1791. I. Title.
BX8495.W5S545   1983   230'.7'0924   83 16721
ISBN 0-8191-3552-6 (pbk.)

To

Mildred

Elaine Patricia

Mark Edwin and

Paul Andrew

BICENTENNIAL FOREWORD

As United Methodist Christians approach the two hundredth birthday of our American connection, we should and will turn again to our roots.

Secular historians acknowledge that in the eighteenth century John Wesley and the Methodists saved England from the equivalent of the French Revolution. The Wesleyan prescription of personal holiness and social righteousness was just what was needed to cure the moral and spiritual disease that had infected England. The same impact was characteristic of the Methodist influence upon the American continent.

Fire In The Brand tells the story of John Wesley's work and helps the reader to reflect upon the theology that produced such amazing fruits in English and American Life.

The organization of the book makes clear the quality of Mr. Wesley's impact through his preaching, his hymns and his influence in the market place.

The theological section is excellent. I am particularly grateful for the creative way in which Dr. Slaatte reflects upon John Wesley's experience and the existential setting from which his theology and ministry emerged. I also appreciate the chapter entitled "The Dialectical Creativity" which reveals Wesleyan theology as a bridge between classical Protestantism and the modern industrial world.

This book is superb. I will read it again and again. I trust and expect that it will become a valuable tool, as we United Methodists examine our roots during the bicentennial celebration.

William Boyd Grove
Bishop
The United Methodist Church

Charleston, West Virginia

FOREWORD

READING the proof of *Fire in the Brand* has proved to be one of the happiest experiences of the year. Dr. Slaatte gets straight to the man in quick order. I have been wanting a book like this on Wesley for years and can hardly wait until I get a copy that I can mark and use.

Without making John Wesley a tool for homiletics, the author has shown the form and style of his preaching in such a way that one wants to follow him. He is pictured as a man of the time and for the time, and a man of the book, but also a man for and with the people. The personal discipline and manners are pictured in such a way as to be avenues of reaching people in a positive way.

The influence of the man on society from the social, economic and theological approaches is seen in his preaching, in his hymns, in his doctrine and in his pastoral outreach.

I was interested in seeing how the existential perspective is brought into the picture as Dr. Slaatte shows Mr. Wesley's faith, method and theology as the balance of the transcendent and immanent. His treatment of Wesleyan beliefs is excellent.

Fire in the Brand is a book that I want to read and reread, and one that will help any person better to understand Wesley and the Methodist movement. If you knew the spirit, purpose and zeal of the author, that would add to your appreciation and admiration. This book needs to be read in its entirety so that you may see the full balance and excellent coverage.

BISHOP PAUL V. GALLOWAY
The Methodist Church

San Antonio, Texas

CONTENTS

INTRODUCTION

THE present study is intended as a convenient introduction to the creative work and theology of John Wesley. As such it is designed to be a cross-section of the more outstanding activities and the mature thought of perhaps the most influential eighteenth-century exponent of the gospel of Christ.

It has been written with a high regard for the climactic change in the life and ministry of John Wesley that is identified with his spiritual experience at Aldersgate. This is given special attention in Chapter IV. Both what precedes and what follows that discussion is given a special dimension of significance from that highpoint in Wesley's life. It is rather fitting that fresh consideration should be given to it at this time, which marks the 225th anniversary of Wesley's Aldersgate awakening.

As a practical introduction to the theology and labors of one of the most effective preachers of the historical Church and the mainspring of the Evangelical Awakening, the understaking is perhaps less original in nature than convenient. The writer is quick to acknowledge his indebtedness to many scholars who have probed the breadth, height and depth of Wesley's background, spiritual development, education, Churchmanship, evangelistic outreach, intellectual perspective and doctrinal position. Should a claim to any originality be made, it lies primarily in the theses propounded and demonstrated in Chapters IV and V concerning, respectively, "the existential context" and "the dialectical creativity" of Wesley's theology. These chapters are not only anticipated in Part One, but provide the setting for what follows in Part Two. Distinctive perhaps but of secondary importance is the cross-section of Wesley's more creative work and basic theology as provided by the outline in general. In Part One the focal points of his work are homiletic, literary and social in nature; in Part Two the perspectives of his theology are existential, dialectical and systematic. Little else may be regarded as original; nevertheless, it is hoped that the fresh approach and con-

cise combination of the highlights of Wesley's work and theology
will prove of value to both the student and the general reader.

The basic outline of this study almost presupposes one's familiarity with the life of John Wesley. Though frequent references are
made to his more outstanding experiences, a brief biographical
sketch may serve as a helpful review and background for what follows.

The life of John Wesley nearly spanned the eighteenth century. He
was born in 1703 and died in 1791. He was the main leader of the
Evangelical Awakening of that century, which stirred the British Isles
and caused conspicuous reverberations on other shores, including
young America. Next in importance in the leadership of that great
movement were his brother Charles Wesley and his good friend
George Whitefield.

John Wesley was born into a well-disciplined home at Epworth,
England, the son of Samuel Wesley, a Nonconformist priest of the
Anglican Church, and his devout, many-talented wife, Susanna. When
John was six years of age, their home burned and he narrowly es-
caped. Thereafter, his mother regarded him as "a brand plucked from
the fire."

In 1714, John went to London and enrolled at Charterhouse
School. He was graduated at seventeen, then went up to Oxford,
where he matriculated at Christ Church. A devout and diligent student, he read widely and became proficient in several languages.
Upon being graduated from Christ Church, he became a Fellow at
Lincoln College, Oxford, in 1726, and was ordained to the priesthood
in 1728.

In November, 1729, he became leader of the so-called Holy Club,
which his brother had formed earlier that year. The nickname "Methodist" was applied to the members because of their disciplined devotional practices. In 1735, George Whitefield joined the group,
becoming a lifelong friend of Wesley, despite their theological dif-
ferences. Whitefield was of a more Calvinistic persuasion. Eventually it was Whitefield who became one of the most effective preachers
in America, known especially up and down the Atlantic seaboard.
(Even Benjamin Franklin felt his influence, and in 1740, together,
the two men founded the University of Pennsylvania.)

That same year, 1735, the Wesley brothers sailed to Georgia as missionaries to the Indians and the young colony founded by General Oglethorpe for German refugees from religious persecution and debtors' prison. On the voyage, and in Georgia, John met several Moravian leaders whose thinking and religious experiences impressed him greatly. But his high-churchly ways did not seem to be a need either of the colonists or of the Indians. After two years in Georgia, he felt that, for the most part, he had failed.

Wesley returned to London early in 1738 with deep-seated misgivings in his soul. One evening in May, he came to the climactic turning point of his life, what is known as his Aldersgate "heart-warming." Basically a doctrinal vivification of hitherto unrecognized personal relevance, this was the inner awakening that led John Wesley to become the great evangelist of the British Isles and the organizer of the Methodist movement. What was this big difference in Wesley's life and ministry? It was his existential awakening to the meaning of salvation by faith, here and now.

After visits among the Moravians in Germany, Wesley returned to England to preach in various societies and churches. His message met with considerable opposition in the established churches, and he often was dismissed as an enthusiast. In a day when a cold deism was mounting, Wesley nevertheless clarified for the people the personal meaning of justification by faith and the Christian holiness of life. His aim was "to spread scriptural holiness" everywhere, based upon divine grace and freedom from sin through love.

Reluctantly but eventually, Wesley turned to field preaching under Whitefield's influence, finding it a boon to the evangelization of the neglected masses. When not endorsed by a local priest, yet mindful of the Great Commission, he chose to preach anyway, under the conviction: "The world is my parish." Persecution often followed, as clergymen, deistic sophisticates and enraged mobs put undue pressure on him to cease his activities. Wesley never wavered, but fulfilled his own dictum: "Always look a mob in the face." As the Word and Spirit of God fairly shook men's hearts and minds, his preaching left cleansed souls and clean sweeps of social impact. In many a community conspicuous forms of debauchery were quelled, as a wholesome hunger for righteousness gripped the people.

Wesley was a remarkable organizer. He established many societies of believers and honest seekers-after-God, who conducted "class meetings" for study, prayer, mutual self-examination and fellowship. Their pattern was the Holy Club, at Oxford. At first, Wesley resisted lay preaching, but later conceded to the visible results of it and took it under his guidance. Lay preaching became another boon to the evangelical awakening of the people.

In superintending his work throughout the British Isles, and preaching more than twice a day on the average, Wesley traveled about five thousand miles a year, mostly on horseback. Everywhere he went he preached, organized societies and spread both scriptural and general literacy. He could have died in wealth had he not reinvested his income from hundreds of writings into more writings and several benevolent causes, including schools and orphanages.

In the course of time, the Wesleyan movement withdrew from the Church of England. Wesley wanted the Methodist societies to become integral to the established Church, if possible, and encouraged members to take communion regularly. But the problem of too few ordained clergy to serve them arose. Thus the matter of ordination also became acute. Maintaining that elders were as much capacitated to ordain as bishops, Wesley, largely out of necessity, opened up a new dimension to the movement that contributed to its separation as a body. As the need for ordained clergy was increasingly felt, especially in the United States, where after the Revolutionary War Methodism spread rapidly, he and Dr. Thomas Coke, another priest, ordained two elders to serve in America. Wesley also appointed Coke and Francis Asbury as superintendents of the work there. In 1784, he made provisions for the continuation of his movement after his death.

Preaching and serving in every way he could until his last days, the great leader of one of the greatest awakenings of history died in 1791, at the age of eighty-eight.

A perusal of the life of John Wesley, and especially of his creative work and theology as contained in the main chapters of this work, is enough to see the power of the Word and Spirit of God at work among men. It is then that we begin to understand something of the providence of "a brand plucked from the fire"—but perhaps even more what constitutes the *fire* in the brand!

PART ONE

WESLEY'S WORK

CHAPTER I

WESLEY'S PREACHING

JOHN WESLEY (1703–1791) was a man of his time and, even more, a man for his time. Very much adapted to his age, he was by no means bound to it. As a leader of men he was very much involved in the course of eighteenth-century events, yet sufficiently above them to be ahead of his time. Not conformed to the world around him, he was transformed by God.

It can fairly be said that this man of the Spirit, a learned but humble scholar, itinerant preacher and founder of Methodism, was gifted with administrative ability and intellectual acumen excelled by none of his contemporaries and few churchmen of history. The assailants of this unpretentious, consecrated and erudite man of God soon learned of his keenness of mind, which was disclosed both in his preaching and in his prolific writings. A combination of evangelist, missionary, scholar, philanthropist, writer, theologian and social reformer, John Wesley was truly a giant of his age.

Few today realize how irreligious were the majority of the people in John Wesley's day. Bishop George Berkeley, the noted philosopher, stated: "The age of monsters is not far off." Wesley himself once commented: "Nine tenths of the men in England have no more religion than horses."[1] In most communities in early-eighteenth-century Britain, religion seemed either a cold matter or something that did not matter. Religious sincerity in that day was deemed fanatical. Freethinking scorn, a stuffy deism, a mounting rationalism and a class-conscious Anglican clergy combined to make religion something almost undesirable, if not irrelevant, to the masses. While bishops rode in carriages attended by servants, the lower clergy nearly starved. Samuel Wesley, parish priest and father of John, knew what it meant to spend months in a debtors' prison.

---

[1] Cited by Oscar Sherwin, in *John Wesley, Friend of the People*, p. 11.

As both Samuel Johnson and Voltaire indicated, the typical sermons of the period were dry discourses, sometimes as polished as marble but equally cold. The Age of Reason had come, and religion was under its constraints. Men were offered no redemption from sin, no dynamic for reform, and but little more than formal renditions of moral platitudes. The choicest texts included "Let your moderation be known to all men" and "Be not righteous overmuch."[2] Bishop Joseph Butler's *Analogy of Religion* had gone too far in contending that "probability is the guide of life." William Law was an exception. He saw that Christianity should not compromise with the rationalistic temper of the day. He also saw how human reason is corrupted by a sinful condition, and that it needs to be illuminated by revelation.[3]

It would take a revolutionary power to stem and turn the tide of such a sterile popular religion. Providentially, the change was realized, however, for into that stream of spiritual apathy and moral and social decadence stepped John Wesley of Epworth and Oxford, an inspired preacher of the Word of God who dared to stand against the evils of the day. It was chiefly through him that "the Ice Age" of religion, as F. Gerald Ensley speaks of it,[4] was melted, and the social climate remarkably changed.

John Wesley was an ardent, provocative and convincing preacher who saw the spiritual needs of the people of his day and strove to meet them. As one who combined the biblical content and the redemptive doctrine with the personal relevance and ethical responsibility of the gospel of Christ, his ministry of more than half a century was one of mature evangelistic and prophetic efficacy. Consequently, Wesley was the main figure in the Evangelical Awakening of the eighteenth century, a movement that fairly shook the English-speaking world out of its moral and spiritual lethargy into a new perspective of vision, hope and responsibility.

What we owe to Wesley is immeasurable, with respect to offsetting the imbalanced rationalism and humanism of the Enlightenment period. He vivified for men in all walks of life the pertinence of a vital

[2] Oscar Sherwin, *John Wesley, Friend of the People*, p. 274.

[3] Arnold Nash, "The England to Which John Wesley Came," in *Methodism*, edited by William K. Anderson, pp. 19 f.

[4] Gerald Ensley, *John Wesley, Evangelist*, p. 9.

faith to their personal existence, even in a society increasingly deper-
sonalized by the Industrial Revolution. Most persons who have taken
a serious look at Wesley's work have been amazed at his accomplish-
ments, and impressed by what a Christ-centered devotion can make
of a man's life. A contemporary likened him to Saint John in character and personality. Like Saint Paul, he was diminutive in stature
but truly gigantic in soul.

"Judged by productive results, the greatest preacher since the
days of Jesus and of Paul was John Wesley," states William C. S.
Pellowe. "His sermons have reformed more lives, lifted more nations,
produced more preachers, missionaries, and Christian workers, released more social regenerative energies, and given rise to more
separate denominations than the sermons of any man that used the
art of preaching as his instrument of productice action."[5] Such an
appraisal—by no means intemperate—can be understood better in
the light of the fact that during his ministry Wesley earned the reputation of being the most successful of open-air preachers, and "a
veritable apostle of the British Isles."

Wesley's work continued from the point where Puritanism had
left off. The gospel as a vitally personal issue was almost strange to
the people of his day. Wesley was intent on helping to vivify the
personal and social relevance of the gospel to men's lives. If people
failed to come to the Church, this meant taking the message to the
people. Reluctantly, therefore, he turned to field preaching at Bristol.
Most people regarded it as an eccentric practice. In fact, Wesley's
own disposition and academic demeanor biased him against it. Only
the striking success of George Whitefield's experiments with open-air
preaching changed his attitude. Whitefield had been his colleague
in the Holy Club at Oxford. "What marvel," Wesley came to say,
"the devil does not like field preaching. Neither do I. I love a com-
modius room, a soft cushion, a handsome pulpit. But where is my
zeal if I do not trample all these under foot in order to save one more
soul?"[6]

Wesley conceded that his earlier high-churchly outlook was too
stiff and unbending; however, by no means did he forsake the role

---

[5] William C. S. Pellowe, *John Wesley, Master in Religion*, p. 15
[6] Cited by G. Holden Pike, in *John Wesley and His Preachers*, p. 2.

of orderly worship and ritual. In fact, he remained a priest in the Church of England until his death. Nevertheless, with Wesley first things had to come first, even if the price had to be nonconformity. Always a man of churchly decorum, he wrote in his *Journal* for March 31, 1739: "I shall have thought the saving of souls almost a sin, if it had not been done in a church."[7] But preferences, he realized, must not stand in the way of the evangelistic task. Yet, in a sense, Wesley submitted to the new method as an expedient, for he had no serious desire to preach in the open until he was prohibited from using the pulpits of the Established Church. Frequently it was a lack of sufficient accommodations that forced him outdoors to preach.

Wesley's basic purpose was to win men to Christ and present them "salvation unto eternal life." The aim of his endeavors and those of the Methodist societies were "to spread scriptural holiness throughout the land." This was to Wesley a dignified responsibility, which demanded a verdict from the individual without anything sensational being involved.

Most of Wesley's preaching was in a simple, classical style. Precisely reasoned, well-outlined and concise, his sermons were replete with biblical content and vocabulary. Almost every other sentence had something derived from the Scriptures, yet his sermons were far from being a patchwork of texts. Never ostentatious, he used the plain, formal English that was common in his day. If a child could understand John Wesley's sermons, as has been asserted, it was due largely to the simple, clear and direct manner of his presentation. Often a brief, terse text provided the theme. He once defined good style thus: "Perspicacity and purity, propriety, strength and easiness, joined together."[8] He applied his definition consistently.

Homiletically speaking, Wesley was a biblical expositor, although not what we usually mean by a textual expositor. His commonest method was to expound a biblical doctrine brought into focus by a brief text, rather than to analyze and expound an extensive passage. Usually three major points germane to the text were announced and unfolded with logical coherence. Eloquence, rhetoric and oratorical finesse were always mitigated and kept obeisant to the content. The

---

[7] John Wesley, *Journal*, March 31, 1739.

[8] Cited by F. Luke Wiseman, in *Charles Wesley, Evangelist and Poet*, p. 201.

message proper was made to stand out above all form. Never was the substance obscured by the architectonics of the preacher.

Wesley's sermons are impressive for their logical appeal and structure, yet not overly intellectual in manner of presentation. This, despite frequent references to the classics and the Scriptures. Wesley saw the need to be communicative and used tact in adapting himself to the occasion on which and the people to whom he spoke. He is reputed to have said that he could no more preach a fine sermon than he could wear a fine coat. But to study Wesley's sermons is to think otherwise, for Wesley is truly an architect of thought, and one who reflects the painstaking skill and art of a guild craftsman. As Pellowe puts it, Wesley's messages are "made with the chisels of reason driven home by the hammer blows of a vital personal experience of God."[9]

As eloquent and dramatic as were his great colleagues John Fletcher and George Whitefield, they were not superior to Wesley in general effectiveness. Calm and coherent, lucid and logical, Wesley moved the understanding of his hearers in a most pleasing and appealing manner. There was something about both his bearing and his simple style that intensified everything he said. Someone once remarked: "His sermon was not masterly, yet none but a master could have preached it."

If men were moved by Whitefield's oratory, with its emotional and dramatic style, they were impressed as much or more by Wesley's penetrating words, with their unmistakable logic and attention-holding directness. John Nelson heard John Wesley at Moorsfield, and said he actually felt his heart beat as the preacher's words, like "a hammer and a flame," seemed to be directed at him alone. Extemporaneous with the aid of an outline, Wesley's repetition of sermons led him often to delete less relevant material, thus enhancing the acuity of every word. At one time rather elaborate in form, he changed conscientiously to a simpler style when he learned that a servant could not understand him.[10] Wesley stated that he wanted plain truth to get through to plain people.[11]

---

9 Pellowe *op. cit.*, pp. 18, 16.
10 Sherwin, *op. cit.*, pp. 86 f.
11 John Wesley, *Sermons on Several Occasions*, Vol. 1 (1794), p. ii.

In the preface to the first volume of *Sermons on Several Occasions* (1794), Wesley states frankly: "Nothing here appears in an elaborate, elegant or oratorical dress . . . for I now write (as I generally speak) *ad populum*: To the bulk of mankind, to those who neither relish nor understand the art of speaking . . . I mention this, that curious readers may spare themselves the labour of seeking for what they will not find."[12] Deliberately, Wesley avoids all speculative and intricate arguments as well as an uncommon vocabulary and evidence of self-conscious erudition. He even states forthrightly: "Nay, my design is in some sense to forget all that I have read in my life."[13] Not to be pressed literally, this is but "in some sense" the case. Actually, Wesley profited much by his extensive reading, and he fostered productive reading among both his fellow clergymen and lay people. But anything ponderous had to give way to what was perspicuous and propaedeutic. Concerned about a lucid communication, never did Wesley wish to impress people more with himself than his message. To preach was to convey his message from his heart, not just his head.

Wesley's typical calmness, as he preached, was not something altogether natural. It was, rather, that of restrained emotion. Sensing that what he said was intensely vital both to him and to themselves, listeners were gripped by his statements, and fairly hung on his words.

An expressed but controlled conviction was to him the true way to men's hearts. Logic and feeling, therefore, were a compatible and effective team. Using his voice skillfully meant that he used it naturally, unaffectedly and moderately. While sometimes Wesley spoke vehemently and with a little extra volume, he never went to extremes. For him the hour of preaching was a "love feast" preparatory to a distinct fellowship.[14]

John Wesley's sermons were always controlled by his logic and his spirit. Seldom metaphorical, he was different in this respect from his brother Charles, who as a poet was much more pithy and aphoristic. John was more of a logician in action, letting the sequence of thought bear major testimony. Though simple in style, he was metic-

12 *Ibid.*
13 *Ibid,* p. iii.
14 Sherwin, *op. cit.,* pp. 87–89, 94.

ulous, explicit and parallel in structure. As the outline stands out, the message becomes a bas relief of clear and convincing beauty. Though seldom philosophical or speculative, Wesley was always theological without being ponderous or technical. Only on occasion was he polemical, as in the case of his sermon on "Scriptural Christianity."[15] Here he became argumentative about the doctrine of the Holy Spirit in relation to the experiences of men of his day as compared with men at Pentecost.

Not dramatic, Wesley was nevertheless dynamic. His dignified fervor and Spirit-endowed personality combined with his doctrinal convictions gave a special quality to both his message and delivery. Preparation and spontaneity seemed to converge under divine inspiration to give a depth dimension to his words. The ring of authority sounded forth not primarily because of how he said things but because of what he said. And what he said was grounded in what the Lord said. Wesley preached the living Word of Life, a redemptive word to all men. Wesley not only preached the doctrine of the Holy Spirit, he *lived* it; he relied on Him in all his undertakings. Thus he preached as a man endowed with an electric power, not of his own creative dynamo, but of the Spirit of the eternal God. He himself once intimated that his message fairly burned within his brain. Little wonder that his general bearing should seem to convey his very message and mission. Even in his earlier ministry, when he preached from his father's gravestone at Lincoln, in June, 1742, a clergyman could not withold saying: "Your presence created an awe, as if you were an inhabitant of another world."[16]

Let there be no misunderstanding: Wesley was no actor in the pulpit. He sought to create no stylized impression in people's minds. He sought only to witness honestly to the meaning of the Gospel, to share its good news and challenge men to see and walk in the way of Christ. When Wesley preached, critical observers noticed ". . . the serenity of his features, the commanding sweetness of his voice, the grace and propriety of his few gestures. They noted likewise the unfolding of his argument, paragraph linked to paragraph by faultless reasoning, for although Wesley's greatness as a preacher was in the

---

[15] John Wesley, *The Standard Sermons of John Wesley*, edited by Sugden, Vol. I, p. 87.

[16] W. McDonald, *The Young People's Wesley*, pp. 136–39.

plainness and loving severity with which he applied the truth, yet
he never applied it until he had unfolded it with the skill of which
his training had made him master. Then, however, he spoke with a
plainness, a directness, a courage, a holy energy never surpassed in
the history of preaching."[17]

Few preachers of history have been accustomed to preach to
larger groups of people with greater attentiveness and more clearly
visible results. There were times when men were literally smitten
by Wesley's preaching. Sometimes among the hundreds and even
thousands of people to whom he preached in open places there even
appeared strange phenomena, but Wesley never catered to them.
Physical demonstrations in the form of prostration, convulsions, or
agony sometimes accompanied the spiritual ∟ iction that came over
people. But always such storms were follow ed by 'le peace and assurance of divine forgiveness and reconciliation. Puzzling to Wesley
himself, the phenomena were assumed to be a part of the methods of
God.[18]

How lengthy were Wesley's sermons? One of the earliest editors
of Wesley's works, the Reverend Thomas Jackson, states: "Those who
judge Wesley's ministry from sermons which he preached and published in the decline of life greatly mistake his real character. Till he
was enfeebled by age his discourses were not at all remarkable for
their brevity. They were often extended to a considerable length.
Wesley the preacher was tethered by no lines of written preparation
and verbal recollection; he spoke with extraordinary power of ut-
terance out of the fullness of his heart."[19] Yet, comparatively speaking, seldom would Wesley prolong a typical sermon without a sense
of purpose, likewise a service of a designated time.[20]

We have come to sense the peculiar powers of address that accompanied Wesley's message; yet nothing artificial could be at-
tributed to them. Though a bit lengthy as compared with sermons of
today, Wesley's were never redundant so as to fatigue his listeners.
His literary qualities, directness, simplicity, logic and lucidity combined matchlessly to spearhead his well-outlined message. Though the

---

17 Charles J. Little, *John Wesley, Preacher of Scriptural Christianity*, p. 14.
18 McDonald, *op. cit.*, pp. 140 f.
19 Cited by McDonald, *loc. cit.*, p. 141.
20 Pike, *op. cit.*, pp. 3 f.

intelligentsia always found his sermons stimulating and enlightening, usually they were directed to the masses. Wesley was gifted with a remarkable insight into human character, men's practical needs and psychological tendencies. Nothing went unnoticed. Everything was seen in the light of his spiritual ambition and outlook as epitomized in his own words: "The world is my parish."

Much of the power of Wesley's preaching lay in the closeness and directness of his appeal to people to be decisive and expressive of their faith. Passionately, yet well poised, he would entreat men to accept Christ, the Gospel and the full responsibility of the Christian life. The conscience of a sinner was bound to be stirred, for Wesley neither underplayed the meaning of sin nor minimized men's need of divine aid. In keeping with his own experience and empirical trends of thought, he let it be known that men of any description or station could experience for themselves the liberating significance of the Gospel and be assured of salvation in the here and now.

We understand better how remarkable it was that Wesley managed to get the common, uneducated people of his day to listen to him, when we realize that the age of the Evangelical Revival was not characterized by the sensational methods and advertising of the modern day. The language of the common man was closer to the biblical vocabulary of the Elizabethan period and the literature of that day. Even the comparatively uneducated masses were more amenable to classical expression. It was also a day when the Bible was respected in general as a book of divine authority. Thus Wesley's scriptural references and classical allusions were accepted more readily than they might have been in later generations. Wesley's sermons abound in classical references, especially those delivered before his more distinguished congregations. This is understandable, for Wesley always adapted himself to the people. Only on occasion would he use anecdotes pertaining to the Chinese or the American Indians, for example, or a few illustrations from his knowledge of electricity. Always positive rather than negative, Wesley was not given to playing on men's emotions, nor did he accentuate the fear of hell; rather, he appealed to men concerning "the beauty of holiness." On the other hand, he made room for hell, especially when attacking a hypocrisy that feigned immunity from judgment, because of, say, one's social station or even baptism. One sees this clearly in his sermon "The Marks of the New Birth."

Wesley's message is thought to have been so fresh and pertinent to men's lives that "it needed little illustration in order to keep people interested."[21] Of course, the copies of his sermons available to us today do not convey the personal effects of his presentation. We wish we had a few tape recordings and movies of his work, but alas! There were times, however, when he was not so well prepared as usual. Not typical of him, these sermons were padded with more anecdotes than usual. In general, his sermons possessed a vitality that made them far superior to the dry discourses and insipid mouthings of deistic pulpiteers devoid of spiritual depth, like so many heard in the average parish of that day. Undoubtedly his evangelistic and ethical passion intensified his words, together with his homiletic style.

As for the more explicit features of his form or style, we find that Wesley used little variation. The introduction to his sermon is usually general and, only a paragraph in length, it contains the thesis or topic. Upon being first announced, the major points of the outline are taken up and subpoints treated in detail. This is the body of the sermon. An example of his three-point sermons is "The Witness of the Spirit." A rarer, two-point sermon is "The Almost Christian."[22] The exposition and logical argumentation supported by concrete material is commonly followed by a vivid conclusion. Usually the conclusion is a pointed and powerful personal exhortation for commitment in the light of the main ideas discussed. This form is simple, direct and meaningful. It was an ideal instrument for the impartation of his message to educated and uneducated alike. It was an appeal for a verdict, a commitment, a showing of colors.

Thus, in the close of his message, Wesley "comes to grips with his audience like one wrestler gripping another for the throw to the mat." He is not content with preaching that does not provoke, inspire, or convict people to a definite response. For him, even a negative response is better than none at all. He saw in his way what Sören Kierkegaard enunciated a century ago in Denmark: No decision is

---

21 Pellowe, *op. cit.*, pp. 16 f.

22 John Wesley, *Sermons on Several Occasions*, Vol. I (1853), p. 126; also Sugden, *op. cit.*, p. 53.

still a decision. Or, as Jesus said: "He who is not for me is against me." The story is told of how Wesley would question the preaching of a new man in the field. "Did he win anyone to Christ?" If the answer was negative, a second question was asked: "Did he make anyone angry?" If both questions were answered negatively, Wesley would say that the man was not really called to preach!

As reflected in his sermon "The Great Assize,"[23] for instance, Wesley repeatedly states a warning that must have made a mark upon the consciences of the judges and other public dignitaries to whom he was preaching. The element of decision and responsibility cannot be missed. "The object of a Wesleyan sermon was not to reach an oratorical climax but to sensitize the nerves of men's consciences, to energize their wills, to bring them, penitent, humble, hungry, in sight of the Cross."[24] Yet this is not to be understood as something achieved by the repetition of platitudes, clichés or something similar accentuated by an emotional pitch, mob psychology or sentimental picture. Not at all! John Wesley saw that heart and head must work together, that reason is a servant of religion—though not her master—wherever the faith perspective is mature.

It should *not* be surprising that Wesley was positively against so-called gospel preachers who, he said, "corrupt their hearers and vitiate their taste."[25] For Wesley, preaching the Gospel called for much more than an emotional appeal. "I am sick and tired," he once frankly remarked, "of hearing some men preach Christ. Let but a pert, self-sufficient animal, that hath neither sense nor grace, bawl out something about Christ or his blood, or justification by faith, and his hearers cry out, 'What a fine gospel sermon!' "[26] This position of Wesley's is corroborated by his painful break with the much-respected Moravians, whose emotionalism, especially among their hymn writers, he could not condone.[27] Sensitive to the harm done by preachers with poor taste and a slushy, sentimental message, Wesley said: "They feed them sweetmeats till the genuine wine of the

23 Sugden, *op. cit.*, Vol. II, p. 398.

24 Pellowe, *op. cit.*, p. 23; cf. pp. 20–23.

25 Cited by Little, *op. cit.*, p. 16.

26 Cited by Luccock, Hutchinson and Goodloe, *The Story of Methodism* (1948), p. 18.

27 Cf. *infra*, Chapter III.

kingdom seems quite insipid to them. They gave them cordial upon
cordial which make all life and spirit for the present but meantime
their appetite is destroyed, so that they can neither retain nor digest
the pure milk of the word . . ."[28]

John Wesley adapted his sermons to his congregations. Though
he always preferred to minister to the common people of a given
community, he adapted the depth and tone of his message to the
needs of whatever class, occasion or place visited.[29] It is told that on
one occasion when Wesley spoke to a large number of children, he
did not use a single word beyond two syllables; however, he conceded that he was not a preacher to the people of Edinburgh and that
"he seldom spoke so roughly as when in Scotland." Always moving
from place to place, he preached regularly in prisons and counseled
those sentenced to death. Sometimes the latter were groups of condemned children,[30] imprisoned in that day for things we would deem
to be but misdemeanors.

Wesley was a man of remarkable self-control. For him holiness
was conjoined with good taste and good cheer. Like his colleague
John Fletcher, the theologian of the Wesleyan movement, contro-
versies did not befuddle him to the point of becoming angry or rude.
Even when attacked by mobs he retained his equanimity. Remarkably
challenging to us are his own words in this regard: "If once anger
arises," he wrote, "this smoke will so dim the eyes of my soul, that
I shall be able to see nothing clearly . . . For how far is love, even
with many wrong opinions, to be preferred before truth itself without
love?"[31] That John Wesley applied what he asserted is without question. In this respect an illuminating statement was made by the wife
of his brother Charles upon comparing the two brothers. She stated
of John that his was "a temper which scarcely any injuries could provoke, ingratitude ruffle, or contradiction weary. This disposition
peculiarly qualified him to govern; but he was far from arrogating
authority, or demanding submission, and his gentleness and for-
bearance rendered him so much the object of love amongst the people. . . . The peculiar virtue of John was forgiveness of enemies. He

---

[28] Cited by Little, *op. cit.*
[29] Pike, *op. cit.*, pp. 3–5.
[30] Ensley, *op. cit.*, pp. 56 f.
[31] Wesley, *Sermons*, Vol. I (1794), *op. cit.*, p. vii.

has been frequently known to receive into his confidence those who had betrayed it, and basely injured him."[32]

Such a disposition made Wesley a truly magnanimous person and an understanding spirit. Though gravely concerned about the spiritual life of Dr. Samuel Johnson, for instance, Wesley always admired him as a great man.[33]

This is not to suggest that Wesley was a will-o'-the-wisp who did not assert himself in opposition to those of differing views. He and his brother Charles, for example, agreed to disagree honorably and lovingly on some matters. Charles was always more conservative about ecclesiastical rubrics. On one occasion he threatened to leave the conference if laymen were admitted to the discussion. Whereupon John said to a colleague: "Give my brother his hat." On another occasion he stated: "Soul-damning clergy keep me under more difficulties than soul-saving laymen." "Church or no Church," he once commented, "we must attend to the work of saving souls."[34] To Francis Asbury he once stated: "Men may call me a knave or a fool, a rascal, a scoundrel, and I am content, but they shall never by my consent call me Bishop."[35]

It was not easy for him culturally, but by the time he was sixty Wesley had outgrown his own high-church prejudices and was unhesitant about preaching in unconsecrated places. When past middle age, he still preached about eight hundred sermons a year, the overall average for his ministry being three or four a day. Preaching twice a day besides regular Sunday duties had a "bracing effect" upon him, he said. The older he became, the more invitations were given him, and the more he could not fulfil.[36] At seventy-five, Wesley

---

[32] Mrs. Charles Wesley, Preface to *Sermons of the Late Charles Wesley* (1816), as cited in the Appendix of Wiseman, *op. cit.*, p. 229.

[33] Cf. Pike, *op. cit.*, pp. 5–10.

[34] George Eayres, ed., *Letters of John Wesley*, p. 68.

[35] Sherwin, *op. cit.*, Chapter 6: Yet this might call for elucidation. Wesley's maturest view was that only episcopal ordination was valid but that presbyters and bishops were identical in order, differing only in office or function. The episcopal form of government is scriptural and apostolic, he said in 1756, but not necessarily *prescribed* in the scriptures by either Christ or the apostles. He later states, "I firmly believe I am a scriptural *episcopos* as much as any man in England, for the uninterrupted succession I know to be a fable . . ." As cited by Abel Stevens, *History of American Methodism*, Appendix, p. 586.

[36] Pike, *op. cit.*, p. 16.

felt he had not developed as a preacher beyond his capacity at the age of forty![37]

Wesley always respected the Church year, selecting appropriate Scriptures. When he prepared his sermons he did so on the basis of the original languages. He incorporated parallel passages of Scripture on the same theme as the text. Usually he wrote out his sermons, but preached extemporaneously, sometimes with a few notes. In his earlier ministry he read his sermons, but he dropped that method of delivery when he once forgot his manuscript, only to discover a pulpit liberty he had not known to be possible.[38]

A man of remarkable discipline, John Wesley managed to study up to twelve hours a day under average circumstances, if not in his study, then on his horse or in his carriage. His mastery of Greek, Latin, French, German, Spanish and other languages enabled him to write articles for or against thinkers of other lands. His many books, pamphlets, hymnals, grammars and essays were powerfully bolstered by his grasp of linguistics as well as by his scientific, philosophical and theological acumen.

Wesley's motto was "Lord, let me not live to be useless." Always methodical, and one who never wasted his time, he planned engagements in advance, and after planning his schedule he often went through great difficulty to fulfil his appointments. Almost defiant of any kind of weather, he rarely failed to appear. During his ministry he traveled on horseback more than a quarter of a million miles, resorting to a carriage only late in life. Between 1738 and 1791, he preached no less than 52,400 times, organized and superintended hundreds of societies throughout the British Isles, wrote 233 books and pamphlets, edited 200 others, kept a journal and a diary, edited two magazines and organized many charities, while always ready to give time to those who needed his services, especially the sick and the poor. Preaching at five in the morning was for Wesley an invigorating experience. In times of illness he was never idle. Once he even rose above a serious threat of tuberculosis. An hour each day was spent in devotions, and six and one-half hours of sleep were the

---

[37] *Ibid*, pp. 3–5.
[38] Ensley, *op. cit.*, pp. 43 f.

most he would accept. "The soul and body make a man," he said; "the spirit and discipline make a Christian."[39]

Wesley declared himself to be *Homo unius libri,* a "man of one book," the Bible.[40] This statement must not be pressed literally, however, for, as we have seen, Wesley was widely read and conversant with many intellectual disciplines, discourses, and issues. In fact, he is known to have said: "If you need no book but the Bible, you are not above Saint Paul. He wanted others too." (Cf. II Timothy 4:13.) What Wesley meant was that for him the Bible was the sublime vessel of divine truth, the book supreme because of its indispensable message of divine grace, which men of every age must heed. Actually, Wesley believed in reading extensively in many areas that he might better elucidate the Bible's message. Besides great poetry, the classics and outstanding works in theology, he even read the works of the irreligious romanticist Rousseau.[41] Yet these were not the sources but the tools of Wesley's preaching. Not bookish, he mastered much knowledge that it might be the servant of the Gospel. He specified many great books for his co-workers to read.

Indeed, the greatest source material for Wesley was the Scriptures. Next in importance was the Gospel's relationship to the personal faith experience. To read his sermons is to note how they are constructively saturated with biblical doctrine and verse. "No preacher since the Church Fathers of the second and third centuries ever used so much Scripture to the page as did Wesley in his sermons."[42] To read them is to be convinced. He himself stated that his aim was to preach salvation "with a view to distinguish this way of God, from all those which are the inventions of men." He added: "I have endeavored to describe the true, the scriptural, experimental religion, so as to omit nothing."[43]

Wesley, in large measure, interprets Scripture by Scripture without being a literalist. Sometimes his interpretations are distinctive. In his hermeneutics of the Beatitudes of Jesus, for example, he caters

---

39 Sherwin, *op. cit.,* Ch. 6.
40 Wesley, *Sermons,* Vol. I (1794), p. iv.
41 Cf. Pellowe, *op. cit.,* p. 26.
42 *Ibid,* p. 29.
43 Wesley, *Sermons,* Vol. I (1794), p. vi.

to a Pauline perspective.[44] In many respects he was a shrewd scholar
and critic from both a theological and a literary standpoint. More
than what his sermons might reflect in this respect, his *Notes on the
New Testament* shows this unmistakably, not to overlook his translation of the New Testament. Wesley especially admired not only the
teachings of Saint John but his literary style and pastoral concern as
well.[45] Yet in some respects Wesley was still linked with medieval
views of the Bible, while understandably so, for he was a man of his
time introduced to little, if anything, of what we regard today as the
higher criticism of biblical studies. Arthur J. Little reminds us that
some modern critics who poke fun at Wesley's infrequent reference
to good and bad angels, for instance, forget that "Wesley shared . . .
these beliefs with Shakespeare and Kepler and Bunyan and Bishop
Ken and Samuel Johnson."[46]

In his address to the clergy, which he wrote in 1756, John Wesley
enumerated what he considered to be essential working materials for
a preacher. These were—

1. Knowledge of the Bible.
2. Knowledge of the original tongue in which the Scriptures were
   written.
3. Knowledge of the profane history, ancient customs, chronology
   and geography involved.
4. Knowledge of the writings of the early Church Fathers.
5. Knowledge of the sciences, of metaphysics and of natural philosophy (physics and related cosmic theory).
6. Knowledge of men, their maxims, tempers and manners, such as
   they occur in real life.[47]

Needless to say, these were things which Wesley himself pursued
diligently, both as a scholar and as a minister to men's souls. Most of
these principles are even reflected in single discourses by Wesley. A
good case in point is his sermon "On Original Sin."[48] Here he summons ideas from many areas to support his contention. Wesley's
prayerful, self-disciplined life not only allowed him, but inspired

---

[44] Cf. Wesley, *Standard Sermons*, Vols. I and II, edited by Sugden.
[45] Cf. Pike, *op. cit.*, p. ii.
[46] Arthur J. Little, *The Times and Teaching of John Wesley*, pp. 32–41.
[47] Pellowe, *op. cit.*, p. 23.
[48] Wesley, *Sermons*, Vol. I (1853), p. 384; also *Standard Sermons*, Vol.
II, p. 207.

him, to reckon with almost every conceivable intellectual problem of his day, even as it enhanced his effectiveness as a preacher. A life of holiness for him meant a life of wholeness and consistent dedication to all of God's truth.

How could Wesley do so much? Only by being a methodical "Methodist" who tried to account for every minute and waste none of it. Once, in a letter to an Irish preacher, he listed some things for sincere leaders to practice. Condensed, they were as follows: (1) "Be active, be diligent; avoid all laziness . . ." (2) "Be cleanly." (3) "Let your clothes be neat and whole." (4) "Use no tobacco," a "filthy habit." (5) "Drink no liquor."

Elsewhere Wesley advised his colleagues to observe the following (in abbreviated form): (1) Fulfil all preaching engagements. (2) Be punctual in beginning and ending. (3) Adapt your message to your audience. (4) Choose the plainest texts. (5) Do not ramble. (6) Do no allegorize. (7) Avoid awkward speech and gestures. (8) Avoid all clownishness. (9) Encourage all to sing.[49]

In addition, Wesley advised his preachers to speak naturally with an even voice, though varied according to subject matter; never to thump the pulpit; to be well informed; to read extensively from the classics and the best in philosophy and theology; to distribute books; to be holy and unblamable. Not averse to symbolism or substantial ritual when appropriate, Wesley found kneeling the only manner in which to pray. After-service talk in a sanctuary was not to be condoned.[50]

Wesley believed in, practiced and fostered good manners. He also did concrete things to promote good health, even experimenting with medicines. Besides spreading literature, he counseled some folks about good health, diet and hygiene. It was almost an avocation with him. Ahead of his time in respect to psychosomatic matters, he saw how spiritual health is conducive to mental and physical health. He even recommended to some that they be "electrified" for nervous disorders, thus anticipating the modern shock treatment.[51]

Though highly pragmatic about many things, John Wesley sought truth first and results second. Yet, experience and its effect on peo-

---

49 Cf. Sherwin, *op. cit.*, Ch. 7.

50 *Ibid.*; cf. Pike, *op. cit.*, pp. 17–19.

51 Ensley, *op. cit.*, p. 32.

ple was to him the greatest test of truth, both spiritually and practically. If people preferred to gather at five in the morning for a
preaching service, he was ready to accommodate. Situations contributed much to procedures, hence, Wesley led a remarkably fluid
and adaptable movement, for he set the precedents. Whatever the
situation, it was always his aim to meet his hearers' needs in a four-
fold way: (1) to invite them, (2) to convince them, (3) to offer
them Christ, (4) to edify and build up the fellowship.[52] Wesley was
bent on establishing the societies in almost every community. More
basic than creed or rules was the fellowship that centered in men's
faith experience and spiritual seeking as based on the Word of God.
Liberty of conscience and opinion was always promoted, and no
binding mode of worship was imposed on the societies.[53] Even so,
he recommended good order and designated specific forms and aids.

Theological in all his sermons, only in some did Wesley expound a single doctrine thoroughly as an end in itself. Exemplary is
his sermon "Salvation by Faith," which he preached at St. Mary's,
Oxford, on May 28, 1738, shortly after his Aldersgate experience.
Similarly, his sermons "Justification by Faith," "The Witness of the
Spirit" and "On Original Sin." Some of his sermons closely related
to everyday life have special theological grounding, however, such as
his message on "Conscience."[54] Some of Wesley's sermons are like
spiritual manifestoes relative not only to others but his own experience. This is the case with "Salvation by Faith," preached at St.
Mary's, in which he expresses a more theocentric view than he had
held earlier. It is also the case with his forceful two-point sermon
"The Almost Christian."[55] In the last, Wesley refers to the contrast in
his own life as related to his Aldersgate experience, when he saw
clearly for the first time the difference between salvation by law and
salvation by grace.

A favorite theme for Wesley was the providence of God. Not predestinarian, he nevertheless saw God and men of faith creatively
working together on the divine terms of creation and grace. Grace

---

[52] *Ibid.*, p. 42.

[53] Cf. Luccock, Hutchinson and Goodloe, *op. cit.*

[54] Cf. Wesley's sermon "The Witness of Our Own Spirit," *Sermons on Several Occasions,* Vol. 1 (1794), pp. 213 ff.

[55] Wesley, *Sermons,* Vol. I (1794), p. 25; Vol. II (1853), p. 126.

is primary, however, and God works in all things, whether or not we see them in our favor. A favorite text was "Jesus Christ, who of God is made unto us wisdom, righteousness, sanctification and redemption" (I Cor. 1:30).[56]

Among those printed, Wesley's sermon series on the Sermon on the Mount[57] has been regarded as his best in the area of applied ethics. "Read any one of those thirteen discourses with seriousness, and you will be led on a tour of self-introspection which makes one humiliated at his shortcomings."[58] Wesley also shows great concern for the domestic and social aspects of religion in such sermons as "The Reformation of Manners," "The Education of Children," "Visiting the Sick," "The Use of Money," "On Riches," "The Good Steward" and "National Sins and Miseries."[59] The last would serve as an example of how "the apostle of the English-speaking world" found it important and dutiful to speak on contemporary cultural and political problems and events. John Wesley saw Christian salvation to be no escape from the world, with its oppressing problems, but as including the desire to reckon with them in hope and love. Wesley's insistence that good works are the fruit and evidence of true faith made his preaching all the more effective. He made it clear that a faith-conditioned righteousness was as active as it was passive, as productive in the Spirit as it was receptive of divine grace.

As a preacher with a shepherd's heart and an evangelist's passion, Wesley had a message of universal appeal. To him all men were subjects of the saving grace of God, all sinners potential saints, when brought under the Word and the Spirit. Always, any seeker after God, whether he had professed to have found God or not, was welcome to join the Methodist societies that Wesley founded. "If thy heart is as mine," he said, "I give thee the right hand of fellowship." While doctrinally concerned, never did Wesley insist on a dogmatic conformity, or let anything take priority over the spirit of a thought, group or task. "Think and let think," he is known to have said. Exceedingly significant was his pastoral sympathy for any and all repentant sinners and sincere seekers. Another characteristic was his

---

56 Cf. Little, *op. cit.*, pp. 8–11.
57 Wesley, *Standard Sermons*, Vols. I and II, *op. cit.*
58 Pellowe, *op. cit.*, p. 21.
59 Wesley, *Sermons*, Vol. II (1853) ; also *Standard Sermons*, Vol. II.

ability to remain calm in the face of disturbing circumstances, whether it was sorrow, the sting of false accusations, or the threats of a violent mob.[60] "Always look a mob in the face," he said: This he did more than once.

Never satisfied with his public ministry, Wesley not only preached to the people, but followed his efforts with personal contacts as a good shepherd of the flock. He had the true pastoral touch. Not blind to his defects, he tried earnestly to live the doctrines he preached, never expecting others to do any more than he himself fulfilled. In fact, he usually superseded his recommendations to his co-laborers. Always he expressed his loving concern for the poor and the under-privileged, as he led men to actuate their Christian love for God and neighbor. This is reflected in the many gifts, writings, social efforts and philanthropic endeavors that he undertook. He believed that if men were to be saved they must understand salvation in its fullest sense, not only *from* sin but *to* the new life. Not a negative religion, when understood and experienced from within, it was positive both in its uplook and its outreach. Thus Wesley loved to quote in his sermons the apostle's words, "the faith that works by love."

Wesley had a simple faith in his calling to preach the Word of God wherever he could do the most good. Though his message burned within him as something precious to be shared, he really did not like the itinerant type of life to which the grace of God had constrained him. Wesley believed himself to be "a priest of the Church Universal," and like Peter and Paul preferred to be obedient to God rather than men. His fairly diminutive frame and sensitive throat proved most serviceable, as faith was combined with care. Charles J. Little has expressively stated: "Seldom has anyone taken so little thought for the morrow; seldom has anyone seen so clearly and fought so bravely the evil of the day; seldom has anyone so daringly placed first the kingdom of God and the righteousness thereof; seldom has anyone so confidently expected God to vindicate the conduct of an honest servant by giving increase in his labor."[61]

Wesley symbolizes the true role of preaching the Word as an indispensable means of divine grace to men of all ages who need a God

---

[60] Cf. Pike, *op. cit.*, pp. 17–19.
[61] C. J. Little, *op. cit.*, pp. 5 f.

much bigger than themselves. The eighteenth-century society to which he came was one of a groping, but frustrated people. The Awakening that he led showed them new possibilities under God. When men learned of a saving God who cared, they began to heed the great proclamation of the cross. When they heard of a saving experience for each and all, they came seeking that they might find. When men accepted it in Christ, they yielded to his Spirit and sought his will and way. Culturally, it was this that made the witness of Wesley one of the most tide-turning forces in history. We still feel the impact of the Word of God as preached by this Oxford don, who allowed God to use him as a consecrated vessel, by which divine grace was channeled to the thirsty souls of a misled and parched generation. Thus it was that the desert sands of a humanistic self-sufficiency were thrust back by a God-ordained oasis, which became a flowering plain under the preached Word seen relevant to all of life.

CHAPTER II

WESLEY'S HYMNOLOGY

JOHN WESLEY is known particularly as a preacher, a writer and an administrator. His brother Charles is known mainly as a hymn writer. Nevertheless, it can be stated that John Wesley was as much a hymnist as his brother, perhaps more so.

John Wesley's place among outstanding hymn writers and hymnologists is commonly underestimated. Usually it is Charles who is credited with being the spearhead of Wesleyan hymnody, but this needs some qualification, for John deserves special recognition as the promoter and editor of some of the most outstanding innovations in all hymnody. In fact, as Frederick John Gillman concedes:

> John Wesley and not Charles stands at the fountain-head of Methodist hymnody. He was the first in the field, and his directing and controlling hand was never withdrawn. He saw more clearly than any man since Luther the propagandist value of song as an aid to the evangelist.[1]

Actually, John Wesley greatly influenced his brother Charles as a hymn writer. Referring to the work of Charles, J. B. Reeves says: "Surely no verse writer had a more enthusiastic and energetic Maecenas than he."[2]

Though it would seem that John Wesley should have been too busy as a preacher, writer and organizer to write many hymns, he still managed to translate dozens of hymns from Latin, German and Spanish. He was an exceptional linguist, and even wrote Hebrew, Greek, Latin and French grammars for his schools at Kingswood and Newcastle. He also compiled and published a handy English dictionary, along with writing more than one hundred works and serving as editor of *The Arminian*, a magazine.[3] A friend once said

[1] Frederick J. Gillman, *The Evolution of the English Hymn*, p. 217.
[2] Jeremiah B. Reeves, *The Hymn as Literature*, p. 166.
[3] Cf. Oscar Sherwin, *John Wesley, Friend of the People*, pp. 145 f., 150, 158.

of Wesley: "He had a fine taste for poetry and composed himself many of our hymns, but he told me that he and his brother agreed not to distinguish their hymns from each other."[4]

On October 14, 1735, Bishop David Nitschmann of the Church of England set sail from London with twenty-six others to evangelize the Creek and Cherokee Indians in America. Of this voyage Winfred Douglas, an Episcopalian, states: "On the same ship were two young Anglican Priests, John and Charles Wesley, whom God raised up to revive in the Anglican Communion a life which was being choked by formalism, frigidity, and Erastianism."[5] John and his brother were accustomed to singing hymns in the meadows near Oxford. They brought along several volumes of hymns for personal and corporate worship. On the third day of the voyage John began to study German, in order to converse with the Moravians who were aboard. Within a few weeks he began to translate Count von Zinzendorf's *Gesangbuch*, the songbook used at Herrnhut, the music and words of which greatly affected him. Expressively, Douglas states:

> Thus, on the tossing Atlantic, German and English traditions blended in the heart and mind of a young high Churchman who was to startle the Anglican world with a spirituality which depended upon personal, individual experience: and John Wesley was to bring about a practical eclectic. Hymnody which neither Coverdale nor the editor of *Lyra Davidica* had been able to achieve.[6]

During the journey to America, John Wesley usually studied German from nine in the morning till noon, and joined the Germans in an evening service at seven, so by January, 1736, he could freely converse with them. James Hatfield tells us: "February 6, 1736, they landed near Savannah, and the next day Wesley met Spangenberg, the well-known Moravian pastor, and spent several days in conversing with him about his experiences, and about the Moravian church at Herrnhut." In the archives at Herrnhut, Germany, Hatfield found an interesting unpublished document; it was John Wesley's first letter

---

[4] Reeves, *op. cit.*, pp. 179 f.

[5] Winfred Douglas, *Church Music in History and Practice*, p. 232. "Erastianism" refers to the supremacy of the state in ecclesiastical matters.

[6] *Ibid.*, p. 233. Cf. below *re* Miles Coverdale.

to Count Zinzendorf, written in Latin and closing with the first allusion to a German hymn in any of Wesley's writings:

> Einen Helden muth
> Der da Gut und Blut
> Gern um deinet willen lasse
> > Gieb ihm, Hochstes Gut,
> > Durch dein theures Blut![7]

Just a year and a day after he began to learn German, Wesley recorded in his *Journal* that he had begun to hold special services every noon for the Germans at Frederica who could not understand English.

When Wesley began his missionary work in America, he also began a more intricate study of hymns. His assiduous study sometimes continued through the working hours of several successive days. Carefully he selected several hymns for his American work, especially the hymns by Isaac Watts. At Savannah and Frederica, Wesley introduced hymn singing, even including them in Sunday church services.[8] In Georgia, John worked diligently to prepare a hymnal for local use. It was printed anonymously at Charlestown and entitled *A Collection of Psalms and Hymns.*

In August, 1737, Wesley was charged before the grand jury with altering the metrical psalms and "introducing into the Church and service at the Altar compositions of psalms and hymns not inspected or authorized by any proper judicature." Actually this book was the first Anglican hymnal.[9] While still in manuscript Wesley had tested the collection by reading the hymns to his friends, and by using them for sickroom and group devotions.[10]

Strange to say, it was not until the close of the last century that it was learned that, in 1736, John Wesley prepared the first hymnbook of the Anglican Church. Before that time the Church of England had no hymnbook. Psalms metrically rendered by Sternhold, Hopkins, George Herbert and Jeremy Taylor were in circulation, and hymns were included in devotional books, but there was no hymn-

---

[7] James T. Hatfield, *Translations of German Hymns*, p. 5.
[8] Louis F. Benson, *The English Hymn*, p. 225.
[9] Douglas, *op. cit.*, p. 235.
[10] Benson, *op. cit.*, pp. 225 f.

book as such. In 1882, in a London bookstore, a copy of the *Collection* printed in 1737 at Charlestown by Lewis Timothy was found. John Wesley undoubtedly arranged for its publication when he and his brother Charles went to Charlestown on July 31, 1736. In it were John's translations from German hymns, mostly Moravian; poems by his father and his brother Samuel; other poems by Addison and Herbert; and hymns by Isaac Watts.[11] Altogether the book contains seventy hymns, thirty-one by Watts, six by George Herbert, ten by the Wesleys and five translations from the German by John Wesley—the first in this class. The only indication of their source are the words "From the German."[12]

Not long after John Wesley returned to England, his brother Charles also returned and experienced his spiritual renewal on Whitsunday, 1738. About this time John met a Moravian student, Peter Böhler, and later visited the Moravian colony at Herrnhut. He attended their services and love feasts, heard them sing many hymns of praise and saw them go through the streets singing the Gospel to their neighbors.[13] Earlier in 1738 Wesley became a member of the Moravian society in Fetter Lane, London. It was under the guidance of its members that he came to a more vivid faith in Christ. The high point was what he described as his "heart-warming experience" at Aldersgate, London. Though earlier the members of the Holy Club at Oxford had been labeled "Methodists," it was really this high point that launched the Methodist revival, "which was only lost to the Church," says high-churchman Winfred Douglas, "through ecclesiastical blindness and folly."[14]

Hymn singing became popular with the Wesleyan revival. Its novelty and expressiveness strengthened men's faith both doctrinally and experientially. John soon enlarged his American hymnal, and it was probably for the use of the Moravian society that he published in London, in 1738, his collection *Psalms and Hymns*. This volume is extremely rare, there being only three copies known. It contains no names, but there are five more German translations.[15]

[11] Douglas, *op. cit.*, p. 236.
[12] Hatfield, *op. cit.*, p. 7.
[13] Gillman, *op. cit.*, p. 218.
[14] Douglas, *op. cit.*, p. 236.
[15] Hatfield, *op. cit.*, p. 7.

It was when John Wesley visited Herrnhut, in Germany, that he translated part of Count von Zinzendorf's well-known hymn *Seelenbrautigum*, omitting expressions more characteristic of human love than of divine, which he felt were beginning to weaken Moravian hymnody. It was largely because of their overemphasis upon the physical sufferings and wounds of Christ that Wesley eventually broke with the Moravians. Significant also is the fact that John never included in his collections his brother's most noted hymn, "Jesus, Lover of My Soul," since he, John, deemed it too emotional for general use.[16] Charles, the author of more than six thousand hymns in all, often wrote in a rapturous, romantic and vivid manner. But John often tempered the work of his brother Charles with a more vigorous and precise style.

In 1739, John Wesley's *Hymns and Sacred Poems* first appeared. Twelve new translations of German hymns were included besides the previous ten. In 1740, a new and independent volume, also called *Hymns and Sacred Poems,* was published by John Wesley in London; it contained six more German translations but no reprints. In 1742, a third volume of the same name appeared containing the last of the twenty-nine German translations by John Wesley. After that he translated only one German hymn, since it was in 1740 that a complete separation came about between the Moravian and Methodist societies. James T. Hatfield says:

> In an essay on "Count Zinzendorf and the Moravians," Professor F. H. Hedge referred to five of these translations as "the favorites of our worshipping assemblies" and "precious contributions to our stock of devotional poetry," grouping them all under the title "Moravian," and failing to give Wesley credit. Professor Hedge is only so far right in giving them this title in that Wesley became acquainted with the originals of all of them in Moravian collections. 25 were in the Herrnhut *Gesang-Buch* of 1731 . . . 4 are derived from later appendices to the *Gesang-Buch* of 1735, one from the *Gesang-Buch* of 1737.[17]

It may be noted that the Moravians did not create all of their hymns. Since their church under Zinzendorf was a product of the pietist movement within the Lutheran Church, they adopted many from this

---

16 Douglas, *op. cit.,* p. 236.
17 Hatfield, *op. cit.,* pp. 8 f.

tradition. Fourteen of the twenty-nine hymns earlier referred to are
from hymn writers of the pietist movement, including Paul Gerhardt, C. F. Richter, Freylinhausen, Dessler, Gotter, Ernst Lange,
Joachim Lange, Rothe, Winkler and Gmelin. Wesley also translated
a few hymns by the pietists Tersteegen, of the Reformed Church, and
Scheffler, a Roman Catholic. Of the Moravian hymns, Wesley took
one from Spangenberg, one from Anna Dober and six from Zinzendorf.

These facts also help to confirm the belief that "Methodism stands
in very close relation to German pietism, and is, in some degree, the
descendent of the work of Johann Arned and his spiritual succes-
sors."[18] Wesley translated only one German hymn after his separation from the Moravians, so by 1743 this phase of his work was done.
He opened a field, however, that, by the end of the next century, had
contributed a great body of translated sacred poetry to English-speaking congregations. As T. W. Herbert says of Wesley: "He had wid-
ened and deepened a channel which was to have a great, if not altogether measurable effect upon the whole range of English poetry."[19]
In all, John Wesley, with the aid of his brother, published fifty-six
hymnbooks and several tunebooks.

John Wesley also translated the Paul Gerhardt hymns, "Give to
the Winds Thy Fears" and "Jesus, Thy Boundless Love to Me." The
very quality of his soul and source of his faith are reflected in his
translation of Gerhardt's "Befiehl Du Deine Wege."[20] While he lived,
none of John Wesley's hymnbooks ascribed the German translations
to him, but the argument for his authorship is as follows: (1) All of
them appeared first in books published by John and Charles Wesley.
(2) No evidence has come to light that Charles ever used German.
(3) The translations do not occur in editions of Charles Wesley's
hymns. (4) Charles Wesley's daughter averred that they were versions by her uncle. (5) As early as 1736 John Wesley quotes one of
the hymns in the original. (6) John was unquestionably the com-
piler of the volume in which the first five of them appeared, in 1737.
(7) An extant letter written by a Mr. Molther in 1740 thanks John
Wesley for the English version of Rothe's hymn, translated at his

18 *Ibid.*, p. 9.
19 Thomas W. Herbert, *John Wesley as Editor and Author*, p. 53.
20 Reeves, *op. cit.*, pp. 182, 184.

request. (8) In one of John Wesley's sermons, dated 1789 and entitled "Knowing Christ After the Flesh," he says that he translated many of the Moravian hymns "for the use of our own congregations."[21]

Psalm singing had been introduced into England through the influence of the followers of Luther and Melancthon, when such men of the Reformation as Miles Coverdale (1487–1569) translated German hymns. But the German influence on hymnody ceased until Wesley again tapped this rich source. The translations not only are used by Methodists but are found among at least one hundred important collections, except the Roman Catholic. Noteworthy is the fact that the Church of England has made as much use of Wesley's hymns as many other branches of Protestantism.[22]

At first, Wesley's hymnals did not receive acceptance by other religious bodies, but he published many collections of hymns by outstanding writers, the foremost being the *Psalms and Hymns* of Isaac Watts. Other books contained hymns by several noted hymnists, including Doddridge, Newton, Toplady, Cowper, Stewart, Watts and the Countess of Huntingdon. Wesley revised several of the hymns and improved their poetry.[23] Speaking of Wesley's translations of German hymns, Thomas W. Herbert raises the problem of emotional expression, stating:

> Wesley himself employed that violent Scriptural metaphor of self-abasement so dear to eighteenth century pietism. Quite consistent, however, with his willingness to hear worshippers call themselves worms, was his emphatic denunciation of a familiar or sensuous approach to Deity. His preachers received many a rebuke for bold, irreverent, improper expressions in prayer, especially for the "amorous" manner of supplication. So also in his translations of hymns he avoided following the original into irreverently sensuous imagery . . . Many a kiss and fond embrace failed to appear in his English versions.[24]

Pertaining to this matter Wesley himself stated in his sermon "Knowing Christ After the Flesh":

---

21 Hatfield, *op. cit.*, pp. 9 f.
22 *Ibid.*, p. 10.
23 Reeves, *op. cit.*, pp. 184 f.
24 Herbert, *op. cit.*, p. 51.

Perhaps some may be afraid lest the refraining from these warm expressions, or even gently checking them, should check the fervor of our devotions. It is very possible it may check, or even prevent some kind of fervor which has passed for devotion. Possibly it may prevent loud shouting, horrid, unnatural screaming, repeating the same words 20 or 30 times, jumping two or three feet high, and throwing about the arms or legs both men and women, in a manner shocking not only to religion, but to common decency; But it will never check, much less prevent, true, scriptural devotion. It will even enliven the prayer that is properly addressed to Him, who though he was very man, yet was very God; who, though he was born of a woman, to redeem man; yet was God from everlasting and world without end.[25]

Thus we begin to see how Wesley repudiated a misdirected use of emotion and emotional imagery. No artificial devices or sentimental slush could be condoned. In a letter to his brother Charles he not only warned against extreme "enthusiasm," but asked him to delete a couple of nativity hymns from a collection being printed, calling them "namby-pambical."[26]

Scholars are uncertain of the scope of John Wesley's share in the voluminous output of hymns of the Wesleyan revival. It is generally thought that he handled the German translations and left the writing of most of the English hymns to his brother, yet he criticized his brother's work, which he highly regarded, before it was sent to the press. Seldom did he encourage any of his helpers to write hymns except his brother. He is reputed to have said: "Were we to encourage little poets we should soon be overrun."[27]

John Wesley's contributions to hymnology simply cannot be measured. Jeremiah B. Reeves has said:

John Wesley possessed what has been called the "hymn sense" to an admirable degree. In the precarious business of amending and revising hymns, he changed many of those he published, usually to their sure improvement. The hymns both of Watts and his brother Charles he altered with a bold hand and with a delicate judgment.[28]

25 *Ibid.*, pp. 51 f.
26 John Wesley, *Letters of John Wesley*, edited by Eayres, p. 80.
27 Gillman, *op. cit.*, pp. 218, 229.
28 Reeves, *op. cit.*, p. 182.

John Wesley had a rival in the hymn writer Augustus Toplady, who embraced the doctrine of election. Noteworthy is Toplady's hymn "Rock of Ages," which was not widely known until half a century later.

The form and content of John Wesley's work as a hymnist may now be considered. As a poetic translator and interpreter of hymns, Wesley's work is characterized by simplicity. Though the German originals employ a great variety of meters, which often seem artificial, Wesley "holds to his personal taste and to the genius of English hymnody, by confining himself to the strength of regular forms, and by using no feminine rhymes whatever." He aims at the heart, though not the letter of the original writings, ignoring all artificialities. His tendency to be terse, neat, and compact made for the condensation of material which Zinzendorf so diffusedly wrote. All filler, repetition, padding, meaningless epithets, and cant phrases are avoided. Weak stanzas that reiterate expressed ideas are omitted. Wesley also abhorred broadness in expressing theological ideas, therefore in his hands Gerhardt's "O Welt, sieh hier dein Leben," for example, shrinks from sixteen stanzas of six lines each to a more explicit nine stanzas of four lines. Wesley translated only five of the original hymns stanza for stanza. The average number of stanzas in the original form is twelve; in the translations only eight. Usually the stanzas correspond, and without overlapping. Only once did he change the order of the stanzas.[29]

Wesley's deliberate omissions are noteworthy. They are made on the following bases:

1. *On theological grounds.* Terms and phrases relating specifically to the constitution of the Moravian Brotherhood are eliminated. A reference to chasing away evil spirits by making the sign of a cross is omitted. Wesley does not introduce Satan so frequently as the German pietist hymn writers.

2. *On grounds of rhetoric and taste.* As Hatfield expresses it: "Wesley had a well-developed British repugnance to the sensuous metaphors of certain forms of pietistic poetry." This is seen, for example, in the second of the hymns he translated for the reason that the theme of Christ as bridegroom of the believer is used too freely

---

[29] Hatfield, *op. cit.*, pp. 11 f.

throughout the entire hymn, which begins with the words *Reiner brautgam meiner Seelen.* Using but six of the thirty stanzas, John Wesley omits this intimate familiarity. In 1749 Wesley attacked the hymnbook published by the Moravian James Hutton, since he carries sensuous expressions too far. In place of terms like *Glaubenskuss* Wesley uses "arms of faith," for *Braut* he uses "love," and for *ausser Mund* he uses "enlivening voice." Writes Hatfield: "Commonplace, prosaic, trivial or coarse expressions, and overloaded metaphorical language, are all foreign to the translator's taste . . ." More reverent than *du hast dir was Schlectes zum Lustspiel erlesen* is Wesley's sentence: "How vast Thy love, how great Thy Grace."

Wesley disliked mixed metaphors, and yet he could be extremely literal when he chose.[30] Hatfield says of him:

> Not inconsistent with the simplicity of Wesley's style, but very characteristic of the nicety which was so prominent in his nature, is his fondness for neatly-balanced phrases, for building up well-worded climaxes, the latter feature not being lacking in his models, Winkler (10) and Gerhardt (15), and perhaps somewhat due to the artificial models prevailing when he was so conspicuous a student at Oxford.[31]

Examples of John Wesley's ingenuity of phrase are the following:

> . . . who less
> Than nothing am.

> Grieved with thy Grief, pain'd with thy Pain,
> Ne'er may I feel Self-Love again.

> Yet vile Affections claim a part
> And thou hast only half my heart.

Of Wesley's true poetic gift Hatfield significantly states:

> There is a freshness and spirit in handling the original which makes these hymns masterpieces of translation, not unworthy to be compared in this respect with Luther's versions of the Hebrew psalms. As an original poet, Wesley's chief trait is loftiness, majesty, the "great style" at its full height, never becoming florid or bombastic. Again and again we mark the swelling of the deep Miltonian organ-tone, where the original shows a much less exalted strain.[32]

---

[30] *Ibid.,* pp. 12–15.
[31] *Ibid.,* pp. 16 f.
[32] *Ibid.,* p. 18.

Wesley's style is exemplified by an opening line,

> *Der Konig ruht, and shauet doch,*

which becomes

> High on His Everlasting Throne,
> The King of Saints his Works surveys.

In place of superlatives or repetitions John Wesley effectively uses "a felicitious climax." For example, in place of *Hochstes gut*, he beautifully writes "my Lord, my Life, my All." Wesley's excellent style is due mainly to his extensive knowledge of the Bible and its sublime Hebrew poetry.[33]

John Wesley also wrote paraphrases and adaptations of religious poems by George Herbert. To Wesley these poems were important, because George Herbert had a deep sense of personal fellowship with God, something Wesley wanted to foster among all men. However, poetically, Wesley felt it necessary to "recast Herbert's irregular lines of various lengths into more normal stanzas." When the original adhered to a simple order of meter, Wesley accepted the form, but he did not care for Herbert's shift from eight to four lines, which he frequently employed.

Wesley's favorite verse forms were the tetrameter and trimeter; he avoided the dimeter and pentameter, which he apparently felt were not suited to hymn tunes. His claim to commendation as a poet is seen in his conciseness and simplicity. As Wesley himself wrote in the Preface to his hymnbook of 1779, he used no doggerel, patchy rhymes, bombastic expressions or cant phraseology. All words used are simple, yet meaningful and elegant.[34] His clarity and simplicity replaces the obscurity in George Herbert's poem, "The Elixir":

> All may of thee partake:
> Nothing can be so mean,
> Which with his tincture (for thy sake)
> Will not grow bright and clean.

Wesley makes it read:

> All may of Thee partake:
> Nothing so small can be,

---

[33] *Ibid.*, pp. 20 ff.

[34] Sherwin, *op. cit.*, pp. 159 ff.; cf. Herbert, *op. cit.*, pp. 52–55.

> But draws, when acted for Thy sake,
> Greatness and worth from Thee.

Wesley avoided calling the mind to dwell on "the metaphysical conceits," as T. W. Herbert calls them, wherein the reader must pause and reflect upon the full import of an allusion. For example, George Herbert in "Virtue" writes:

> Only a sweet and virtuous soul,
> Like seasoned timber, never gives;
> But though the whole world turn to coal
> Then chiefly lives.

which Wesley adapts thus:

> Only a sweet and virtuous mind,
> When Nature all in ruin lies,
> When earth and heaven a period find,
> Begins a life that never dies.

Wesley also modernized archaic words found in hymns and poems. Always he was meticulously careful that no irreverence to God in the slightest degree should be seen in any works. It is not known whether any of these poems were sung in early Methodist meetings, but they may have been used for private devotions. Not even all the hymns written by Charles Wesley were meant for singing. Many of them probably appeared in the *The Arminian*,[35] the magazine edited by John for the spiritual and doctrinal edification of the Wesleyans.

We have come to see how John Wesley was the fountainhead of Methodist hymnody, since he really governed the Methodist use of hymns. He showed much confidence in his ability to improve other men's hymns, yet in speaking of the hymns he and Charles wrote, he interestingly said: "Hymn-cobblers should not try to mend them. I really do not think they are able."[36]

An example of John's re-creation of Watt's hymns may be noted. The first lines of one hymn are:[37]

> Nations, attend before his throne,
> With solemn fear, with sacred joy.

---

[35] Herbert, *op. cit.*, pp. 55–58.
[36] Reeves, *op. cit.*, p. 171.
[37] Herbert, *op. cit.*, pp. 62 f.

which Wesley changed to the generally accepted:

> Before Jehovah's awful throne,
> Ye nations, bow with sacred joy.

John Wesley knew, sang, and greatly appreciated many German and English melodies that a congregation could also heartily sing. The fault of most hymns up until his time was their dullness. Wesley began to print the tunes without harmonies for general use, since he thought it best for an entire congregation to sing the melody. Not only did he select the tunes for the hymns, but he actually taught Methodists how to sing. Often he would stop the congregation while singing and ask them questions about what they just sang, in order to promote increased spirit and conscientiousness in singing. Referring to this, Winfred Douglas says: "If our clergy would dare to overcome their conventionality and do likewise, our worship would be the better. John Wesley's great influence was always against the cheap, the showy, the sentimental, the unreal in the music of the hymns, as in their words."[38] Wesley was not a skilled musician like Luther, but he laid down some good rules for Methodist singers. Condensed, they are as follows:[39]

1. Learn the tunes.
2. Sing them as printed.
3. Sing all. "If it is a Cross to you, take it up and you will find a Blessing."
4. Sing lustily and with a good courage.
5. Sing modestly. Do not bawl.
6. Sing in time. Do not run before or stay behind.
7. Above all, sing spiritually. Have an eye to God in every word you sing.

Wesley told the Conference of 1768: "Beware of formality in singing, or it will creep in on us unawares." He disliked florid singing and the "distractions of counterpoint."

Some of the tunes found in Wesley's *A Collection of Tunes Set to Music as They Are Commonly Sung at the Foundry*, printed in 1742, were composed by John G. Lampe, former bassoon player at Covent Garden Theatre, who was converted under Wesley.

---

[38] Douglas, *op. cit.*, p. 237.
[39] Gillman, *op. cit.*, pp. 294 f.

In 1761, there appeared "a quaint-looking forerunner of the modern hymn-and-tune book" entitled *Select Hymns: With Tunes Annexed: Designed Chiefly for the Use of the People Called Methodists.* Its purpose was to preserve the tunes in common use at the time. The first part contained hymns, the second tunes. Wesley worked on this publication for twenty years, receiving little help from the masters of music, because he wanted to present the tunes as they were then sung, whether good or not. One stanza of a hymn was interlined with the unharmonized melody; for the remaining verses one turned to the first part of the volume. He ordered that these tunes be sung as printed and learned before others.[40]

Doctrinally, the Wesleyan hymns served as "the catechism of Methodism." They kept the teaching content before people's minds. The terrors of hell are seldom alluded to. Through them, joy was characteristically expressed in "conscious redemption" and the "striving after a spiritual goal." Even hymns dealing with death and judgment were "songs of triumph or contentment," and the end of penitence was always expressed as hope. In 1860, Dr. James Martineau, the distinguished Unitarian theologian, wrote that the Wesley Hymnbook *A Collection of Hymns for the Use of the People Called Methodist* (1780), a work that sold by the millions, was to him "the grandest instrument of popular religious culture that Christendom has ever produced." This shows that Wesley's hymns had power to attract the various branches of Protestantism.

Earlier, in 1753, when the idea that Methodist societies might become a separate sect was developing, John Wesley began his protest against separation by publishing *Hymns and Spiritual Songs, Intended for the Use of Real Christians of All Denominations*, which included Toplady's "Rock of Ages." In 1787 *A Pocket Hymn Book* of the same type was published by Wesley.

Thomas W. Herbert states, with good insight:

> The occurrence of John Wesley's name in the index to musical composers in certain modern hymnbooks, though it is a merited tribute to his versatility, is likely to mislead some. He deserves recognition for his contributions to church music, not on account of any original work . . . but because of his activity in popularizing other

[40] Herbert, *op. cit.*, pp. 70, 65–69.

men's music, in stimulating musical compositions for religious
purposes, in editing tune-books, in gathering and standardizing a
few popular tunes, and in governing the style of singing which made
Methodist congregations famous.[41]

So Methodist hymnody became more than a body of church songs.
Few have realized the importance of the hymn as a means of religious
instruction more clearly than John Wesley. As he himself said of the
famous *Collection* of 1780, it was "a little body of experimental and
practical divinity" and contained "all the important truths of our
most holy religion."[42] In the words of Louis F. Benson: "The experiences are primarily the Wesleys' own. But it was a feature of
their method to anticipate, and in a remarkable degree to evoke,
in their converts a repetition of their own experiences."[43]

It must be said that the work of both John and Charles Wesley set
a new standard in hymnody on its literary side. Their hymns are
more in accord with the earlier devotional poets than with Isaac
Watts. Says Benson: "They controverted Watts' canon of hymn writing and laid down a new one—a hymn should be a poem." Watts
insisted that hymns should be kept outside of poetry, "stripped of
poetic suggestiveness," whereas John Wesley maintained that the
hymn should be a religious lyric, and that it need not be brought
down to the level of the masses, but, rather, should help lift the masses
to the level of the hymn.[44]

In the present *Methodist Hymnal* there are five translations by
John Wesley and one original hymn by the founder of Methodism.
The original hymn is "We Lift Our Hearts to Thee," the music of
which is based on a chant by Garrett Wellesley.[45] To show its simple
but provocative expressiveness, the first verse of this beautiful hymn
may be quoted:

> We lift our hearts to Thee,
> O Day-Star from on high!
> The sun itself is but the shade,
> Yet cheers both earth and sky.[46]

---

41 *Ibid.*, pp. 63 f., 65.
42 Gillman, *op. cit.*, p. 28.
43 Benson, *op. cit.*, p. 249.
44 *Ibid.*, p. 252.
45 McCutcheon, *Our Hymnody*, pp. 62–64.
46 *The Methodist Hymnal*, no. 36.

In conclusion, it may be said that the more familiar one becomes with the life and work of John Wesley, the more intriguing becomes his great personality. To begin to estimate his effect upon Christendom and the world as a whole is impossible; in fact, his contributions to Christian hymnology alone are immeasurable. Yet John Wesley's work as a hymnist is either overlooked or minimized by the average churchman. Wesley's burning conviction that there were tremendous possibilities in the people's participation in the worship of Almighty God was basic to his deep concern for hymns and their place in worship. What if there had been no John Wesley? What if there had been no John Wesley with deep concern for a recovery of evangelical principles and for the rightful function of hymns? Would there have been an outstanding hymn writer named Charles Wesley? Would the hand of God in the grip of the Evangelical Revival have shaken the world so vigorously into a new Christ-consciousness? How much Living Water would have flowed over the dam of modern hymnody if "the fountain-head" of Methodist song had not been tapped and channeled? Only God knows.

SELECTIONS FROM JOHN WESLEY'S HYMNS

1. Written by John Wesley himself.

We lift our hearts to Thee,
O Day-Star from on high!
The sun itself is but Thy shade,
Yet cheers both earth and sky.

O let Thine orient beams
The night of sin disperse,
The mists of error and of vice
Which shade the universe!

How beauteous nature now:
How dark and sad before!
With joy we view the pleasing change,
And Nature's God adore.

May we this life improve,
To mourn for errors past;
And live this short, revolving day
As if it were our last.

To God the Father, Son,
And Spirit One in Three,
Be glory; as it was, is now,
And shall forever be.   Amen.

2. Translated by John Wesley from a German hymn by Count Nicolaus L. Zinzendorf (1700–1760).

O Thou, to whose all searching sight
The darkness shineth as the light:
Search, prove my heart, it yearns for Thee;
O burst these bonds, and set it free!

If in this darkness wild I stray,
Be Thou my Light, be Thou my Way:
No foes, no violence I fear,
No fraud, while Thou, my God, art near.

When rising floods my soul oe'r-flow,
When sinks my heart in waves of woe;
Jesus, Thy timely aid impart,
And raise my head, and cheer my heart.

Saviour, where'er Thy steps I see,
Dauntless, untired, I follow Thee:
O let Thy hand support me still,
And lead me to Thy holy hill!   Amen.

3. Translated by John Wesley from a German hymn by
Paul Gerhardt (1607–1676).

Jesus, Thy boundless love to me
No thought can reach; no tongue declare;
O knit my thankful heart to Thee,
And reign without a rival there!
Thine wholly, Thine alone, I'd live,
Myself to Thee entirely give.

O Love, how cheering is Thy ray!
All fear before Thy presence flies;
Care, anguish, sorrow, melt away,
Where'er Thy healing beams arise:
O Jesus, nothing may I see,
Nothing desire, or seek, but Thee!

In suffering be Thy love my peace;
In weakness be Thy love my power;
And when the storms of life shall cease,
O Jesus, in that solemn hour,
In death as life be Thou my guide,
And save me, who for me hast died.   Amen.

CHAPTER III

WESLEY'S SOCIO-ECONOMIC INFLUENCE

JOHN WESLEY, in large measure, was not only an effective preacher, administrator and writer but a social reformer as well. This was because his religion, which kept him in touch with the eternal edicts of God, also kept him in touch with the temporal affairs of men. The Wesleyan outlook was not altogether otherworldly, for in looking up it looked ahead and around as well. In fact, Wesley would not have been the creative preacher and theologian that he was, had he not been concerned with both the souls and the societies of men. For him, human existence and destiny were interrelated.

Wesley expressed great concern for the practical problems of this life. Not only did he have an above-average knowledge and interest in the science of his day, notably things pertaining to electricity and medicine, but he was much concerned about the political, social and economic issues that affected the welfare of most men of his time. Many of his writings were directed specifically toward contemporary issues. But perhaps of greater importance is the community of consecrated people whom he led, some of whom were leaders in specific socio-economic reforms of great impact. Wrote Kathleen MacArthur: "The Wesleyan Revival is an outstanding illustration of the efficacy of the combined force of religion with ethics in locating anew the fundamental values of life and in realizing them in the activities and experiences of the common people."[1]

Though the Wesleyan movement was based on experiential and theological footings as reflected in the previous chapters and specified in Part Two, its influence was of immeasurable ethical and social importance, some features of which are still felt to this day. Wherever it gained a foothold, the moral, social and even economic impact was

---

[1] Kathleen Walker MacArthur, *The Economic Ethics of John Wesley*, p. 12.

witnessed. Many people of subsequent generations have hardly realized what they owe to this phase of their Christian heritage. One aspect of the movement was the deliberate propagation of ideas that
would definitely affect areas of secular activity through a fresh interpretation of Christian ethics. Not simply abstract theories, these
were concrete issues vitally related to eighteenth-century society in
England, Ireland and America. Sociologically and economically, they
were far more widespread than what may be confined to denomina-
tional or Church history.[2] One thing people of our day can well afford to review is what they owe culturally in this respect to people
of earlier periods, who did unpopular but ethically progressive things
out of burning convictions of a religious nature. They were not conformed to their environment; they were sufficiently transformed by
the Spirit to apply their principles to the social issues and problems
of everyday life. Such people refused to let the world around them
mold them into a stagnant, artificial existence; rather, they chose to
help remold the world in terms of its greater possibilities under God.

As W. J. Warner expresses it: "The unique genius of the religious awakening was to affect a new moral status for the individual
in his social relationships, and it prescribed a method the effectiveness of which measured the soundness of its insight."[3] The converted
individual's experience would eventuate, through a changed outlook,
in making the divine purpose central to life, and free from evil
tendencies. The test of this achievement would be "the habitual disposition to love that expresses itself in service to the common welfare."[4] This would eventually affect the social order at large.

In a discourse on the Sermon on the Mount, John Wesley stated:

. . . Christianity is essentially a social religion, and that to turn it
into a solitary religion is indeed to destroy it . . . When I say this
is essentially a social religion, I mean not only that it cannot subsist so well, but that it cannot subsist at all, without society—
without living and conversing with other men.[5]

To this leader and the followers of the Evangelical Awakening of the

---

[2] W. J. Warner, *The Wesleyan Movement in the Industrial Revolution*, pp.
56 f.

[3] *Ibid.*, p. 59.

[4] *Ibid.*, p. 71.

[5] *John Wesley, The Works of*, Vol. V; *Sermons*, Vol. I, p. 296.

eighteenth century, "religion was the be-all and end-all of life, and to exclude it from any department of human affairs was to maim and deform it." Furthermore, as J. W. Bready states it: "The current modern notion that the Evangelical Revival was ridiculously individualistic and morbidly otherworldly is completely false. Human fellowship, cooperation and service were at its heart, and pulsed through all its life."[6]

The age in which Wesley was born was one of almost inconceivable debauchery. The moral character of the nation was diseased. The unhappy colliers of Bristol married and murdered freely, while the criminal code was utterly inhumane and the prisons filthy. The Wesley brothers knew what it was to witness children awaiting their turn at the gallows. Gin was "the curse of the poor," drunkenness a national vice. Every sixth house in London was a public house where one could get drunk for a penny, dead drunk for two pence, and have free straw to lie on while recovering. Moral purity was old-fashioned. Gambling was the rage, bull-baiting and cock-fighting entertaining, and child labor common everywhere. In the mines of northern England children began at the age of four to work from sunup to sundown. Few of the peasants and commoners could read or write. In short, as Wesley said, men were unhappy because they were unholy.[7]

In the face of this social decadence Wesley gave men a message of "free grace" that spelled both liberation and equality for all. A saved soul and its saving were social matters, as Wesley saw it, for no man lives unto himself. Christianity was as social as it was personal. The fellowship of common folk in the Methodist societies was voluntary, class leaders being picked from the group. Only a positive religious experience or desire of it was required for joining the societies, together with an ambition to live righteously in accord with the rules.

Brother helped brother. Leaders of the working class were trained from within. In fact, most of the first trade-union leaders were Methodist class leaders.[8] Thus, in historical setting, the rise of Meth-

---

[6] J. W. Bready, *England Before and After Wesley*, p. 202.

[7] Oscar Sherwin, *John Wesley, Friend of the People*, Chapter 1.

[8] This was first called to my attention personally by Dr. Wearmouth, whom I met in the British Museum, in 1950.

odism belonged to the Industrial Revolution. Large sections of the
working population in manufacturing areas turned to Wesley's message. Here was an adaptable communion that kept up with population
shifts, melted the barriers of a segmented society, fulfilled a missionary outreach and offered both dignity and learning to the individual. To the miners of the north, this was not only a form of religious dissent but religious and cultural hope, a ray of light in the
dismal darkness.[9]

Wesley promulgated a religion that relentlessly pressed its way
into the lives of men so as to affect noticeably the way they lived.
Frequently Wesley, in his preaching and writing, referred to the
many practical affairs in life; however, "neither negative goodness,
nor legal observances, nor fulfillment of the demands of common
morality can be passed off for religion with him."[10] In the words of
W. J. Warner, "At no point did early Methodism display its mood
more enthusiastically than in that part of its enterprise devoted to
temporal interests. Its ideal was a quality of life vitalized by a religious motive, but present benefits remained in the foreground."[11]
A new philanthropy was born, leading to reformed prisons and penal
laws, social resistance to slavery, and the first incentives toward popular education. Concern for a future life was not an excuse for
neglecting the present life.

The Revival had a decided effect upon material success. First, the
type of character it produced was fitted to succeed in the pursuit of
gain. The qualities of Christian character that resulted from a new
found faith in God made for the ideal worker; hence such people,
even though poor, were sooner or later more likely to gain wealth. By
applying the Wesleyan exhortations to think freely, read and study as
well as work incessantly, live frugally and waste nothing, the average
man was made capable of rising in his particular vocation. Without
question one great contribution of the Revival was its practical emphasis upon the economic virtues and its endowment of followers
with "a special capacity for successful economic enterprise." Second,
the providential "interference" with men's lives was conducive to an

9 Sherwin, *op. cit.*, Chapter 4.

10 MacArthur, *op. cit.*, pp. 76 f.

11 Warner, *op. cit.*, p. 137.

improved economic outlook. "The doctrine of stewardship was more than a theory of moral accountability. It was a doctrine of an immediate providential preoccupation in material as well as spiritual processes." The providence of God would enable the true Christian to succeed economically. Success was even "a mark of divine approval."[12] Whether completely acceptable today in a theological sense, there was much in that day to endorse the thought.

Wesley inculcated in the minds of his followers the "industrial virtues" of which the Puritans had almost made a religion, and which laid the foundation for improved economic adjustments. Readily perceived by the people, the economic virtues were such things as persistence, prudence and diligence in business, thrift, temperance, honesty, hygiene and self-reliance. All these were especially practical in the light of the new opportunities, as well as the new problems, afforded by the industrial age. These principles had a most perceptible influence upon the neglected groups of miners, colliers, iron workers and the lawless creatures who were a positive menace to British society at that period. Until the rise of Wesleyanism no religious or charitable institution had sought significantly to help these people.[13]

The typical eighteenth-century notions about poverty were not held by the Wesleyans, but resisted. In their day it was common to think (1) that poverty was due to economic necessity, that is, enough could not be produced in a community to enable all to live comfortably; (2) that poverty was not the consequence of bad environment but persisted because poor people were "indolent, preferring debauchery and idleness," unless compelled to work; and (3) that poverty was thought to be "the will of Providence." To the contrary, the Wesleyans more intelligently saw poverty as an economic problem due to specific failure, the result of actually living contrary to divine purpose. They believed that the causes of poverty consisted of "inequitable consumption of products of industry," providing luxuries for the few, while necessities were denied the many. This was immoral, Wesley brought out, for God proposed them to be used by everyone. Poverty was also considered to be due "to the absence of

---

12 *Ibid.*, pp. 159–62.
13 MacArthur, *op. cit.*, pp. 78 f.

the industrial virtues among all classes." The wealthy were more guilty in this respect, since sloth was regarded as a concomitant of luxury and caused unconcern for others. Employment was needed by all people. So the Wesleyan solution called for the practice of Christian ethics, not only in personal life, but in the economic context.[14]

A description of what Wesley and his people rubbed elbows with might be in order:

> In the new industrial towns of the Midlands and the north of England . . . great numbers of people, detached from their own communities, driven from the "land by agricultural changes," and cut off from all social and moral supports to which they had been accustomed, crowded into ever-widening slum areas around the manufacturing centers, and generated vice and violence.
>
> The riots which broke out frequently during Wesley's preaching were, it is true, usually led by someone in a more authoritative station, but the hordes of poor, ignorant, and wretched men were ready instruments to the hands of disturbers and enemies of the religious revival.[15]

Deep concern over this socio-economic problem is expressed by Wesley in a sermon on "National Sins and Miseries," preached November 12, 1775, to the widows and orphans of the soldiers who fell near Boston. Said Wesley:

> That the people suffer none can deny;—that they are afflicted in a more than ordinary manner. Thousands and tens of thousands are at this day deeply afflicted through want of business. It is true, that this want is in some measure removed in some large and opulent towns. But it is also true, that this is far, very far, from being the general case of the kingdom. Nothing is more sure, than that thousands of people in the west of England, throughout Cornwall in particular, in the north, and even in the midland counties are totally unemployed . . . I have known families, who a few years ago lived in an easy, genteel manner, reduced to just as much raiment as they had on, and as much food as they could gather in the field. To this one or other of them repaired once a day, to pick up the turnips which the cattle had left; which they boiled if they could get a few sticks, or otherwise ate raw. Such is the want of food to which many of our countrymen are at this day reduced by want of business.[16]

---

14 Warner, *op. cit.*, pp. 162–65.
15 MacArthur, *op. cit.*, pp. 79 f.
16 Wesley, *Sermons,* Vol. I, pp. 516 f.

John Wesley believed that changed lives would lead to community responsibility, which would be conducive to "fair wages, fair labor, and just economic conditions throughout." Frequently, he urged his stewards and others to be diligent in business. Self-adornment and other forms of indulgence to him were wasteful, and the money spent on these things could have been given to the poor. Luxury was one cause and source of poverty. Men should be sparing in all things, including food and apparel. This would enable more giving to the needy. Economic ills come to both rich and poor because of weak moral conduct, and much of natural suffering was due to downright godlessness.

A man guilty of business conduct that was strictly censured in Wesleyan preaching was quickly removed from the Societies. On the Cornish coast the crime of plundering wrecked ships and robbing and murdering the survivors was common. Wesley held the gentry of Cornwall responsible as plunderers, because they did not enforce the law. This led to an effective social pressure, and by the end of Wesley's career the practice subsided. Wesley and his fellow preachers were strongly against smuggling. It was like stealing, for it dodged the king's revenues. The Wesleyans showed how smuggling indirectly led to higher taxes upon honest man. Persons who did not have the means to pay notes that they endorsed were also expelled from the Societies. "This code of inflexible honesty undoubtedly had much to do with the reputation later gained by the Methodists, who, as the industrial development progressed, were sought after by employers."[17] A contemporary corollary is the "evangelical" Christians in South American countries of our day; they are considered more reliable and trustworthy than most people in their workaday business world.

The Wesleyans also emphasized business integrity, which included the belief that one should not profit from the ignorance or extreme need of others. To sell things only for their value or their usual price was proper. Wesley exhorted his followers to refrain from accepting election bribes. He also condemned the economic slavery practiced by the English in the Indian provinces. Without question, the Wesleyan religion involved the application of Christian principles to daily

[17] *Ibid.*, pp. 80–88, 91.

living and material needs. Nothing could be counted as incidental by
a follower of Wesley. "He is convinced that those virtues which
characterize Christianity most truly are found in social relationships,
and not in the solitary religion . . ."[18] Such an outlook characterized
the true members of the societies, and their Christian social-economic
ideas did much to affect their everyday conduct and that of others.

The practice of the economic virtues was indicative of an interrelationship between religious experience and the industrial and
economic developments of that day. For this reason there was a "correlation between the location of new industrial prosperity and the
success of the most important Methodist Societies." More than that,
"in spirit the affinity of the economic and religious movements was
so close that the vitality of one injected itself into the other."[19] Early
Methodism, therefore, had a definite, pronounced influence upon the
lives of workmen. In fact, the laboring class soon became the larger
part of Wesley's followers. Due both to Wesleyan piety and economic
discipline, they exemplified the highest type of workmen. They were
a people who now personified the moral consequences of religious
experience with traits desirable among workers, whereas the typical
workman of 1755 was described as mentally "abject," "mean" and
"sordid"—a man associated with destitution and indecency. But many
of this type gained true self-respect when they made contact with the
Methodist Societies, which fostered both spiritual liberation and personal independence. As W. J. Warner states: "The supreme economic
virtue of industriousness was being bred into the fibre of Methodist
character and endowed with a moral tone by an intense emotional
experience."[20] Many an objective testimony has verified this.

Several things added to the earning power of families when the
heads of households found religion meaningful to them. Drunkenness
was proscribed, and drunkards were excluded from the Societies.
"The chapel was substituted for the alehouse as the integrater of interests." Homes were saved as lives were changed. In fact, entire communities were sometimes revolutionized for the better.

The thoroughness with which the societies' doctrine of work was
infused into the laboring group of their membership proceeded defi-

18 *Ibid.*, pp. 90–93.
19 Warner, *op. cit.*, p. 166.
20 *Ibid.*, pp. 166 ff., 169.

nitely from the religious motive. No other source could have furnished the driving force of a kind of conduct which established more clearly than any argument the economic consequence of the revival. If it impinged upon the industrial revolution at no other point, its contribution to the ideal labourer's mentality is undebatable.[21]

The religious zeal and daily work of the mechanic, laborer, or weaver became a unified outlook on life. Work was sanctified. Workmen even showed very little self-consciousness in persuading their employers to become Methodists. This reveals the kind of individualism at the heart of the movement. Indeed, the people of the eighteenth century were not slow to recognize the effect of Wesley's teaching on the laboring section of the average community.

Around 1805, Richard Warner appreciatively appraised the work of the Methodist Revival among the Cornish miners. "The witness before the Select Committee on Accidents in Mines in 1835 who credited Methodists with the great changes in the character of the Cornwall miners merely repeated a fact of common knowledge." The Societies had much to do with the reformation of the illiterate Somersetshire colliers. Children and other workers in factories, who were in the lowest social class, were literally transformed. Apprentices who were Methodists became known as the most dependable. The same could be said for tenants who entered the Societies. "Even in the army and navy Methodist soldiers were commended for their steadiness and reliability."

Furthermore, as stated by Warner: "The prominence which Methodists achieved in the iron industry throughout the country was accounted for by that same type of character which made ironmasters disposed to prefer Wesleyans when appointing foremen."[22]

The effect of early Methodism was also stimulating in economic enterprise. Assiduous endeavors to gain and sincere endeavors to save proved the bases for good business. There was a pronounced correlation of religion and business success. "This kind of character was admirably suited to engage in economic pursuits with an initial advantage over other men less persistent, less vigorously self-controlled, and unwilling to be content with a simple and plain standard

21 *Ibid.*, pp. 170, 171.
22 *Ibid.*, pp. 171, 179.

of life." Thus there is little question about the correlation between persons of religiously disciplined character and persons who showed increased material success. Their contemporaries noticed the big difference between them and others and said of the Wesleyans that "Methodists in general are more rich than they were before they became such." This, of course, was due to the same factors that made them dependable workmen. Within a few years some increased their material prosperity many times over. In regard to both tradesmen and workers in industry, the "records are replete with such instances of the temporal fortunes of individual members . . ." Yearly, the number of community leaders throughout England who were Methodists increased. W. J. Warner states pointedly:

> In fact, so pronounced was the observed correlation between the revival forces and economic prosperity that an unfriendly critic of the eighteenth century claimed he had found the key to the great expansion of Methodism in its economic rewards . . . It is convincing testimony to the strength of the religious basis of the movement that the disposition of money was so commonly undertaken in exactly the same spirit of responsibility with which its gain was attempted.[23]

Despite Wesley's theory that wealth tended to rob a man of religion—and which often has proved true—benevolence to the poor, on the part of many prospering Methodists in leading positions in commercial life, increased with their wealth. But, in general, one of the immediate consequences of prosperity among Methodists was a drifting away from the Societies. This, to be sure, was the negative side of the phenomenon. Then, too, there was a changed outlook within the Societies, since in time the rich were prone to dominate, and there was a deviation from earlier, more stringent standards. Gradually, Wesleyanism became "a religion of respectability," but often at the expense of Wesley's original standards. Eventually, followers began to neglect the ideas that all is God's through the community, and that one must not hoard what is really not one's own or bequeath fortunes to one's children.[24]

John Wesley himself made some striking observations on the rapid rise in the economic status of his adherents. Since stewardship

---

23 *Ibid.*, pp. 180–90, 191 f.
24 *Ibid.*, pp. 193–201.

involved all of life, there was such a thing as the "spiritual peril of riches." Wesley observed that Christianity produces not only economic gain but, indirectly, economic effects "adverse to the spirit of Christianity." He noted in his *Journal* that wealth tended to secularize the Revival. Riches and ethical conduct were simply incompatible, he felt. Wesley observed that decay among the Quakers was also due to the accumulation of wealth. In meaning, as George Croft Cell, puts it: "Christianity is thereby necessarily involved in a process of perpetual decay from which it can escape only by a process of incessant revival."[25] Under a system of private property, riches subvert the essence of religion. "The Revival was being rapidly secularized, at least in many societies. And this process appeared to him [Wesley] to be at once the fruit of religion and the cause of its decay. A community brought fully under the dominion of religious forces directed as Wesley directed them will of necessity rise rapidly in its economic status . . . Then the changed economic status had begotten in its subjects a more congenial outlook upon life. And this change seemed to Wesley to be subversive of true religion."[26]

Very important to the Wesleyan economic ethics was the teaching of the value and use of money. In one sermon Wesley said:

The laboring after a large measure of worldly substance, a larger increase of gold and silver,—the laying up any more than these ends require,—it is what is here expressly and absolutely forbidden . . . Consequently, whoever he is that, owing no man anything, and having food and raiment for himself and his household, together with a sufficiency to carry on his worldly business, so far as answers these reasonable purposes; whosoever, I say, being already in these circumstances, seeks a still larger portion on earth; he lives in an open, habitual denial of the Lord that bought him. "He hath" practically "denied the faith," and is worse than "an African or American infidel."

Wesley continued:

A vast majority of them [rich men] are under a curse . . . inasmuch as, in the general tenor of their lives, they are not only robbing God, continually embezzling and wasting their Lord's goods, and, by that

25 George C. Cell, *The Rediscovery of John Wesley*, pp. 363–65, 366.
26 *Ibid.*, p. 379.

very means, corrupting their own souls, but also robbing the poor, the hungry, the naked, wronging the widow and the fatherless, and making themselves accountable for all the want, affliction, and distress which they may but do not remove.[27]

In his sermon on "The Use of Money,"[28] Wesley sums up his teachings on the economic element of religious life by the use of three, probably quoted, points. They are "Gain all you can . . . Save all you can . . . Give all you can." Money was identified with the "mammon of unrighteousness," because it is so often unrighteously procured or used. Too often even Christians fail to heed Christ's admonition: "Lay not up for yourselves treasures upon earth . . ." To gather a surplus is to reject God. Two wrong uses of money, from the Wesleyan standpoint, were storing up money for posterity, and spending it superfluously on oneself. Right uses of it centered about self-support, which included (1) provision for one's family, (2) saving enough to continue to meet one's needs, (3) meeting one's debts and (4) giving to others. These also counteracted the dangers of becoming rich. Money was entrusted to men by God. Men must be stewards. As already seen, Wesley showed deep concern whenever his people became prosperous; he saw the conflict that wealth raised between the "severe ethic" and the alternative of self-enjoyment. The way to prevent Christianity from uprooting itself in this manner was by frugality in all things and by giving.[29] Wesley believed that this principle of charity would "bridge the chasm between monstrous opulence and monstrous misery," but he overlooked the moral injury that charity can inflict upon both classes.[30]

J. Wesley Bready states:

To Wesley, therefore, any enduring antithesis between business and religion was unthinkable. For him the vital question was not, "Should religion interfere with business?" but rather, "How can business avoid going to the devil, if it is not permeated with religious values, and dedicated to religious ends?" Riches, taught this modern prophet, were made for man, not man for riches. Economic ambition, he

---

[27] *Wesley, Works*, Vol. V, *Sermons*, Vol. I, pp. 367 f., 375.

[28] *Ibid.*, Vol. VI, *Sermons*, Vol. I, pp. 126–36.

[29] MacArthur, *op. cit.*, pp. 94–102.

[30] Cell, *op. cit.*, pp. 380 f. Cf. Halford E. Luccock and Paul Hutchinson, *The Story of Methodism*, pp. 192–95 and Francis J. McConnell, *John Wesley*, pp. 247 ff.

believed to be a good servant but an accursed master. The acid test of the economic and commercial life was the query, "To what purpose do the wheels go round?" And unless they moved for the common good, they obviously were out of gear. All "snatching to hoard, and hoarding to snatch" Wesley considered utter insanity. No more than sex appetites, should the acquisitive economic appetites be stimulated or pampered: rather should they be curbed and sublimated to social and spiritual ends.[31]

The Wesleyans were made to understand that a Christian must not save or sell to the injury of another person. Consistently, he must profit only by perfectly honest services. Anything beyond bare necessities should be given to others. Parents should refrain from trying to marry their children with the wealthy. Emphatically, Wesley taught that no money should be earned at the expense of one's health. Usury and pawnbrokery were denounced. Market prices must be observed. To try to ruin a competitor's business to the benefit of one's own was sinful. It must not be overlooked that Wesley himself observed the teachings and rules that he imposed upon the Societies. For example, with the income he made from the sale of his many books, tracts and pamphlets, he could have made a fortune, but he never spent more than thirty pounds a year upon himself. He gave away up to fourteen hundred pounds a year in his usual spirit of love.[32]

Influential to universal material welfare was the fact that the Wesleyan movement was largely confined to the common people. The then rich and influential people were prone to show contempt toward it. As the Bishop of London said, the Methodists were attracting "the lowest and most ignorant of the people." Such an indictment was really a compliment, for the Societies were giving all men religious, social and economic opportunities. All men stood equal before God. Faith removed distinctions, for everyone was in equal need of grace. This provided a basis for the later-to-be-discussed attack on slavery and the manufacture and sale of liquor. In the words of Cell:

It was the impetus given by the Methodist Revival to social reforms and betterment which led the historian John Richard Green to say,

---

[31] Bready, *op. cit.*, p. 234.
[32] *Ibid.*, pp. 236–40.

"The Methodists themselves were the least result of the Revival," and to list among its numerous consequences "a new philanthropy which reformed our prisons, infused clemency and wisdom into our penal laws, abolished the slave trade and gave the first impulses to popular education.[33]

The Wesleyans became interested in the whole of life and developed a social sensitivity. Wesley himself was much concerned about public life and always tried to protect the king's honor, having much to say about civil and religious liberty. He deplored the use of liquor and unjustified Sabbath breaking. In his later life, he and his followers fought for the abolition of slavery. They showed great concern for the necessity of taxes and enforcing their collection, even the British use of force against the Americans. They saw evil in distilling, when there was a food scarcity and unemployment, and luxurious living in the face of starvation. Wesley clearly saw the wrongs of his day and made his people aware of them. Thus Methodism became a movement that overtly devoted part of its expression to the eradication of such evils.

Wesley was capable of showing his people the causes and consequences of economic problems, tracing them to human nature, while not neglecting their other connections. This is disclosed in several significant documents that he wrote, mostly letters to such men as William Pitt, the Earl of Dartmouth, and Lloyd of the London *Evening Post*.[34] As he worked among the Societies he became concerned about the material resources and living conditions of others as well as Methodists. Whenever possible, he helped men by securing jobs for them. His formulated rules of health must not be overlooked. Moderation in diet was strongly emphasized. "He knew nothing about calories, but he hit upon dietary habits that controlled them pretty well." Regularities in the control of the body, and sleep, the efficacy of fresh air, and mental discipline were understood to be important among the Wesleyans. Francis J. McConnell says:

> Wesley was scientific in making place for the control of natural laws. Long after his time men looked upon cholera as a direct scourge from God and insisted that the only way to combat it was by penitence and prayer. Wesley would have admitted, and urged,

---

[33] Cell, *op. cit.*, pp. 367, 368.

[34] MacArthur, *op. cit.*, pp. 102–10.

the need of spiritual resources in such a situation, but he would
have tried to find the natural remedies. At least that is what he was
always striving after for the relief of suffering mortals. It is interesting to read of his researches into knowledge about electricity and
his tests of electric processes on himself . . . which is something of
a proof that his temper was not wholly conservative.[35]

Wesley always tried to make personal contacts with members of
the Societies who were in extreme difficulty. He even attempted to
minister to their bodies, as was necessary in that day. Sickness was
always about him, so he investigated disease and medicine. This became the leader's avocation, and he even published some of his
findings in a work entitled *Primitive Physic*. He compiled for his
people many prescriptions from contemporary doctors. Tar water
was a typical cure-all.[36] Naturally, the meager medical knowledge
of two hundred years ago would not suffice today. But these endeavors contributed to the general welfare of the people.

The early Wesleyan Societies were instrumental in spreading
social righteousness in the general interest and for the welfare of
everyone. This was due much to the interrelationship of religious
experience and material welfare and the stressing of economic ethics.
Definite philanthropic efforts were undertaken by the Wesleyans.
They produced leaders whose influence was immeasurable. McConnell interestingly makes note of this:

> The small Methodist Societies all over England were instruments
> and fields for the development of leaders. Even a class leader, en-
> trusted with the financial and spiritual guidance of a group of not
> more than a dozen persons, was a figure of consequence in the
> Methodist community. The Methodist Societies were training grounds
> in a leadership which might, without Methodism, have been totally
> lost, or never realized or heard of. The leaders trained among the
> Methodists could use their powers and skills in wider fields than the
> specifically religious. When lay preaching became customary, the
> training in public speech of scores of Methodists became a social
> service of incalculable worth . . .[37]

Such Methodist training became noticeable in industrial activities,
especially in the trade union movement, in the first half of nineteenth-
century England. Such leadership was what the world was crying

---

[35] McConnell, *op. cit.*, p. 117.
[36] *Ibid.*, pp. 115–18.
[37] *Ibid.*, p. 237.

for. Noteworthy is the fact that Methodist class leaders were the first labor-union leaders among the miners of northern England.

Much of the leadership potential was directed toward philanthropic causes. A. J. Warner expresses an important perspective of this when he says:

> The philanthropy issuing from the Wesleyan movement was one test of its social theory. Its extent revealed the strength of the movement in moulding social attitudes. Its motives trace the same development in mood and outlook displayed in other phases of the revival. At the same time it demonstrated the weakness of the Wesleyan view as a complete social theory adequate to cope with the problems of the great society.[38]

The actual relief of poverty was believed possible through giving. As early as 1740, just two years after Wesley's Aldersgate experience, Methodist collections fed one hundred and fifty unemployed men each day. Such endeavors were considered to be the "redemption of society by economic means." Bankruptcy was abhorred by Wesley and his followers. To give people work was an economic remedy that would help remove food scarcity and enable people to meet the enormous taxes caused by the national debt. An increased food supply, Wesley stated, would be brought about by the closing of distilleries, which monopolized the corn supply. The price of oats could be lowered by lessening the number of unnecessary horses. To stop all luxury and to discharge half the national debt were also proposed. "Wesley was fearless and unsparing in bringing to the public the distresses of the poor and insistent in his urgency for their relief." In ten years the London Methodists alone contributed £15,000 to "their own poor,"[39] a sum equal to about three to five times as much then as to us today.

Readily, a spirit of spiritual rebirth and social reform made "social democracy" implicit in Methodism. There was a social democracy among the Wesleyans that their leader emphasized, though Wesley did not believe fully in political democracy. He did not believe the people should share in choosing stewards or leaders among the Societies. As Cell describes it:

---

[38] Warner, *op. cit.*, p. 207.
[39] McConnell, *op. cit.*, pp. 247–54.

. . . the exultation of liberal spirits in America and Europe over the advent to power of the rising middle class, only filled the mind of Wesley as it did that of Burke with a feeling of horror . . . Wesley thought and felt in this supreme issue of his century with the conservatives in spite of his ardent popular sympathies and the powerful leaven of social democracy implicit in his message . . . But the sharp-sighted eyes of the ruling classes discerned much better than Wesley himself the democratic implications of his message and the potential social significance of the great religious awakening going on among the masses.[40]

Speaking of the Methodists, the Duchess of Buckingham is quoted as having said that they were "most repulsive and strongly tinctured with impertinence toward their superiors, in perpetually endeavoring to level all ranks and do away with all distinctions." Hence Wesley was scorned in the large Anglican churches and his evangelical message was repudiated.

It is significant that there were no rich men among the Methodists when they organized. "The early Methodists were social nobodies, poor, unlettered, the lowliest folks." So early Methodism was really not so much of a middle-class movement as "a producer of middle classes." Its efficacy led to the elevation of the economic status and mode of living of entire communities. George C. Cell says:

But the naïveté of Wesley's economic ideas and the remedies proposed is most clearly apparent in the fact that he never thinks of increasing surplus and enlarging business with the avowed object and deliberate intent to provide more men with well-paid work and thus elevating the economic status of the workers. He knows nothing of the scientific and systematic organization of free labor as a vocation or business, nor the ownership of capital which such an organization presupposes.[41]

Yet what Cell states here should be tempered by the fact that Wesley was still a man of his day; it was long before scientific economics and sociological analyses of society were known.

Though much of his economic ethics had pertinence, Wesley was not taken too seriously by the rich, because of the weaknesses of some of his proposals. He himself said that in fifty years he doubted

---

[40] Cell, *op. cit.*, pp. 369–71.
[41] *Ibid.*, pp. 371–74, 375.

whether he had convinced fifty wealthy people that covetousness was wrong. Though Wesley failed to promulgate any perfect solutions to the world problems of works, wages, poverty, and property, his observations on them were extremely valuable.[42] His constant voicing of current issues helped make for a thinking religious people, to say the least. This was always associated with material welfare. Members of the Societies took advantage of the changing conditions brought on by the Industrial Revolution in England. By their industry and thrift it was inevitable that they should make material progress, much to the grave concern of their leader. Wesley noted the population trend, in the last half of the eighteenth century, toward and around the factories. In these industrial centers Methodism grew. "At the new industrial centers there was stir and bustle, and the people responded to Methodism in part because it too was stir and bustle. After its fashion, the Industrial Revolution gave Methodism a chance. As a preacher of honest labor for wages and thrift, Wesley helped supply the Revolution with a quality of labor as important as the quantity."[43]

The Wesleyans clung tenaciously to the idea that if all men were converted to God through an inner personal experience of faith, other difficulties—economic, social, and political—would be overcome. Thus in relation to the Industrial Revolution they were also individualistic. Wesleyanism taught the individual the value of securing what he could. "God for every man," on the one hand; "every man for himself," on the other.

The Wesleyans aroused several contemporary leaders to a favorable view of their ethical concerns. Even Lord Shaftsbury, an Anglican, became a leading instrument of group Methodism in its humanitarian aspects. Through him, factory children and chimney sweepers were granted a human chance. Though he was religiously narrow-minded and had little use for democracy, Shaftsbury attacked the industrialists, becoming the instrument by which "the savagery of the British industrial interests was tamed."[44] Methodism

---

42 *Ibid.*, pp. 376–78.

43 McConnell, *op. cit.*, pp. 256–64.

44 *Ibid.*, pp. 265–76.

had at least a threefold social effect on the industrial situation: (1) It helped workmen to discover themselves, lifting them from sordidness to "a higher spiritual world," much to their benefit as workers. (2) It proved Wesley's contention that thrift, industry and frugality would lead to a higher economic status and industrial leadership. (3) It aroused men like Shaftsbury to an awareness of the social and economic wrongs of the new industrial order.[45]

Most of the many philanthropic interests that Methodists were concerned about were achieved personally. Visiting workhouses, prisons, and hospitals to bring a message to the sick, the condemned, felons and the poor were common practices. Charitable projects such as the Kingswood School were inaugurated and Sunday schools were established. Wesley was a supporter of the Strangers' Friend Society and the Humane Society. He also established a loan fund by means of which Methodists helped hundreds of people to secure financial backing for a new business or to further their vocation. Accompanying the obligation that members must not fail to meet with their class each week was the standard that members who could afford it must contribute to the society a shilling every quarter and a penny once a week.[46] The Methodists found the first free medical dispensary in England, in 1746. They raised money to clothe prisoners and bought food, medicine, fuel, and tools for the stricken. Often they housed the aged and secured clothing for the half naked. Under Wesley the Methodists promoted cooperative industry among the poor, and did much to eradicate wretched working conditions. By emphasizing the "nobility of toil and the fraternity of man," immeasurable good was wrought. Much of this was related to the fact that both Charles Wesley and his brother John "helped the masses of England to break forth into song." The spirit of the working class was greatly heightened thereby.[47]

Wesley's preaching of social righteousness must also be considered the application of religion to social and material welfare. Slavery was one of the major issues not overlooked. Wesley's famous tract *Thoughts Upon Slavery*, published in 1774, gave a restrained

[45] *Ibid.*, pp. 292–95.
[46] MacArthur, *op. cit.*, pp. 112–20.
[47] Bready, *op. cit.*, pp. 268–75.

though pungent portrayal of the stark inhumanity of slavery, after which the author penetrated to the moral issues involved. Equally vehement denunciations of slavery appear in other of his publications, in which he reveals the downright disgrace slavery brought upon a nation. Wesley lamented the evils of the slave trade in his *Serious Address to the People of England*, with regard to the state of the nation. This was written during the American Revolution. Six days before his death he wrote a letter to Wilberforce in which he urged him to oppose slavery, calling it "the scandal of religion, of England, and of human nature."

Another social issue that Wesley found necessary to present to the people was the sheer insanity of war. During the Seven Years' War, the Wesleys, in 1758, published their unusual work *Hymns of Intercession for All Mankind*. Writing to Charles, John Wesley, in 1775, during the American Revolution, said that he was on neither side but prayed both for the people of England and the people of America. Soon afterward he wrote the Prime Minister, Lord North, that the Americans would put up a stiff fight, and that they, an oppressed people, only demanded their rights. Writing to Lord Dartmouth, the Colonial Secretary and a devoted convert, in June, 1775, Wesley pleaded for conciliation, warning that the Americans were "ripe for rebellion." During the height of the Revolutionary War he wrote a strong treatise asserting his abhorrence of war and pointing out the poor logic of warfare as a solution of problems. In the autumn of 1775 his emphasis seems to have shifted, for he wrote his *Calm Address to Our American Colonies*, asserting that the taxes they refused to pay were fair. Though this treatise was afterward used in criticism of Wesley, it since has been vindicated by research. Says Bready:

> When therefore the crisis came, Wesley's love of "law or order" made him a staunch defender of Parliament. England's protracted bungling of a delicate situation, he still deplored; but the madness of mobs was a phenomenon with which he was all too familiar; and the provocative outrages of the Colonial mobs, he deemed wholly unpardonable. Hence the famous *Calm Address*.[48]

Consideration of both these issues, slavery and war, was all in the

---

[48] *Ibid.*, pp. 225–28; 229–34, 231.

interest of the general welfare of the people. Without question, the slavery issue especially had an effect in molding the thinking of Methodists and did much indirectly to influence the clash over the problem, several years later.

The Wesleyan outlook on life was spiritualistic yet, at the same time, experimental and pragmatic. "If education means character building and the imparting of ability to live nobly, usefully and cooperatively, Wesley, beyond comparison, was the greatest educationist of his century, and one of the greatest of all time," states Bready. The Methodist Societies encouraged self-help, though often apprenticeship was the means whereby thousands became preachers, teachers, and other leaders. This biblical religion demanded a knowledge of Scripture and books on ethics. The Wesleyans learned much by extensive reading, which was considered essential to genuine Christian living and to moral, spiritual and material welfare. In the interest of cultivating this, Wesley published *The Christian Library* and *The Arminian magazine*. These publications contributed much to popular education, for they encouraged in parents a desire to give their children an education. This led to a steady increase in the number of schools, some of which were supported by the local Societies and some by the United Societies. The Kingswood School was an example of the latter. In fact, the revival also mothered the world-wide Sunday-school movement.[49] This movement was launched in the United States about 1830.

The early Methodists made distinctive contributions to the burgeoning Industrial Revolution, but not to its inception. The reason that the Industrial Revolution occurred when it did lies elsewhere. It was rather that "the English people came in the epoch of the Protestant Reformation under certain influences which impelled them not only to overturn all barriers, but also to blaze the way to industrial freedom . . . [and] they advanced to a distinct superiority in industrial and commercial energy." They were influenced by "the ideal aims and forces by which men were guided in the utilization of the material conditions of life." Not only that, but men won the right to work, vote, and worship as they so desired. The idea of "vocational idealism," or vocational "calling" in civic,

---

[49] *Ibid.*, pp. 265–68.

social, political or economic fields, was distinctively Protestant. Thus Wesleyan appraisal of the economic virtues was similar to that of the Calvinists. The spirit of vocational idealism—of life given entirely to God's call—was even expressed in worship. For example, "the spirit which made of religion a business and of useful labor a religion, found classic expression in Charles Wesley's immortal hymn, rightly called the Marseillaise of Methodism." This hymn, "A Charge to Keep I Have," was written "not for priests and prelates, but for coal miners and carpenters, managers and merchants."

Wesleyanism, a faith including action as a tenet, maintained: "Idleness slays." A man's vocational calling was a part of his service to God. George Cell has characterized this outlook thus: "Life, work and duty become synonyms." Surely, nothing could be more beneficial to an industrial change and progress than that. As Wesley himself explained, Methodism was entirely an incentive to "national industry." And something else that was new: even the services were held at the most convenient times, and the members were urged to in no way neglect "temporal concerns." Pursuit of reasonable gain was "a sign of active faith and continuance in grace." In one of his sermons Wesley makes it clear that to sleep an hour more than one's body requires is serious, for it throws away six hours a week and "hurts your substance." Stewardship in itself was regarded as materially beneficial, for the necessary keeping of accounts revealed waste and inspired rational expenditure. Alcoholism and even tea drinking were regarded as impairments of health and drains upon one's income. Many people were led "to keep the balance on the right side of the ledger and so were started right economically." Eventually, these factors contributed to the capitalistic motive of investing surplus, despite the religious dangers it implied.[50] The Industrial Revolution, without question, was greatly influenced by many a Methodist's surplus. More concretely, we see the enormous influence of Wesleyanism upon the Industrial Revolution in these words of Kathleen MacArthur:

> . . . because of the powerful ethical force of Wesley's teaching, it made good men, trustworthy, dependable, sought after by iron-masters and textile merchants of England's rising industries. These were

---

[50] Cell, *op. cit.*, pp. 395–412.

men instructed in the Wesleyan ethic of work and its doctrine of wealth, endowed with the virtues of sobriety, industry and honesty, ready to take their places in the industrial world.[51]

The genuineness of this great Wesleyan contribution to man's material welfare becomes even more striking when it is noted that Hugh Price Hughes once said that the Wesleyan preachers were the first since the Franciscan friars to have ever reached the working class. To them the teachings were a "gospel of spiritual opportunity" that affected all the material aspects of life.[52]

A criticism is now in order. We can hardly overlook the fact that Wesley "believed so implicitly that a changed man would change his environment that he never considered whether a changed environment might not help to change a man."[53] Here lies a weakness that has been overlooked in the past, but that has received much consideration in recent decades; nevertheless, this by no means minimizes the positive contributions of Wesleyan ethics to social and material welfare. The followers of Wesley discovered, beyond description, that everything in life, including the materialistic, is a part of religion. Succinctly, Kathleen MacArthur expresses it thus: "The foundations of Wesley's ethical teaching may be said to be: individual effort, the moral imperative, the religious impulse."[54] This is very much the case, though the order might better be reversed.

In conclusion, it may be said that the early Wesleyans showed the world that, under conditions that are morally valid, all social and economic activities are divinely sanctioned. This reveals the very close relationship between religious experience and all phases of material success. Man becomes a spiritual steward; therefore there is a very specific relation between religious experience and economic, social, and political well-being.

---

51 MacArthur, *op. cit.*, p. 132.
52 *Ibid.*, pp. 132 f.
53 *Ibid.*, p. 117. MacArthur quotes M. Edwards.
54 *Ibid.*, p. 124.

PART TWO

WESLEY'S THEOLOGY

CHAPTER IV

THE EXISTENTIAL CONTEXT
OF WESLEY'S THEOLOGY

IT CAN BE contended that Wesley's theology had not only an experiential relevance to man, but an existential context, or setting, within his own experience and person. His climactic spiritual experience at Aldersgate, London, is the center of this issue, for not only did it mean Wesley's spiritual liberation and renewal, but his theological **reorientation as well. This is** something too often overlooked by commentators on Wesley's work and theology.

Aldersgate was a revolutionary turning point in Wesley's life and ministry precisely because it was a vivid moment of encounter with the living Word of Life, which shed new light on all of his thought. In short, it was a doctrinal clarification, with marked existential pertinence, to a struggling man of sincere piety that made the Aldersgate experience so significant. This is important, not only in understanding what gave rise to Wesley's most creative work, but in doing justice to both the dialectical creativity and the doctrinal content of Wesley's theology, which will be treated in subsequent chapters. It is imperative, then, that we examine the implications of this contention, in view of what led up to Aldersgate, what took place there and what followed, theologically speaking.

Wesley arrived at a practical and highly experiential type of theology, yet one that was far more than naturalistic or strictly empirical. Even though man was given a significant place in the total picture, Wesley's theology did not admit a religion based on any authority that men might devise. His mature theology was thoroughly theocentric as to its authority and redemptive source, while being anthropocentric in its appeal and demonstration both in personal and social relevance. If preaching and theology were not both biblical in foundation and practical in application, Wesley could see little value in them. Very few opinions could be retained unless they were validated by the witness or testimony of experience. In respect of the latter, Wesley reflects the broad influence of John Locke and the rising school of empiricism. He was strongly empirical in outlook, but not to the point of endorsing Locke's explicit epistemology. Though he appealed to experience, he did not hold that the world exists only as experienced through the senses.[1] Wesley's empiricism was of a broader type; it saw the whole school of experience, or *all* that the concrete self experiences, to be tributary to knowledge. And this, to be sure, not only moved beyond sense perception, but included the distinctive relevance of religious experience as based not simply on human nature, but on faith in God and his revelation, particularly in the New Testament gospel.

As a theologian Wesley was especially creative for his day in having introduced the empirical method into theological reasoning. Perhaps more than any thinker before him he integrated the doctrines of the New Testament and historical Christianity, with their concrete meaning, into personal life. Wesley was much concerned with this bipolar view of the objective and the subjective meanings of the Word of God. He was a thinker who desired to communicate the divine message to the mind of his day, and this ambition was intensified by his awareness of the unprecedented criticism, skepticism, and growing scientific outlook of the age. This, in turn, gave occasion and support to his refusal to lay claim to an infallible system; the truth of God was for him infallible, but man's interpretation of it was not.

A glimpse of the more personal existential elements in the development of Wesley's theology is very much in order, especially if we are better to understand what we mean by the existential context of his theology. Like any other person, Wesley was greatly conditioned both by his religious background and cultural environment and his concrete experience. No person can jump out of his own skin, as it were; he cannot escape the conditioning factors that contribute to his concrete selfhood; he is too much involved existentially for that. Not only does this apply to the cultural and religious atmosphere that Wesley had breathed throughout his youth, as the product of an

---

[1] Umphrey Lee, *John Wesley and Modern Religion*, p. 123.

Anglican rectory and as a student and teaching fellow at Oxford, but it pertains very much to his own religious experience and its interpretation. This, in turn, sheds a special light on his developing theology.

In his earlier years, John Wesley was considerably under the influence of an Anglicanism that had become largely moralistic in thought and pious attitude. The tenor of the times was that Christianity was largely synonymous with good works or good living. Wesley was by no means immune to this trend, and it is reflected frequently in the pages of his *Journal*. The preached message and the sacraments were commonly regarded as supplementary aids at best, if not dispensable, in the thought of the average parishioner. But wherever the New Testament religon was taken seriously, the tendency still was to think in terms of a devout life based on a disciplined pursuit of a righteousness pleasing to God. As good as it was, the motivation was still meritorious in principle. Partly under the influence of his mother, young John accepted these moralistic and legalistic assumptions, though qualified by a more mystical piety that was given precedent in his home.[2] By and large, faith at this time was interpreted by Wesley to be a devout, prayerful striving for the good life. This made faith a form of good works, an act of man rather than a gift of God.

The trend in Wesley's day was to think of man as morally free in a predominantly Pelagian sense, so that at best it was a freely chosen faith that led to righteousness. Obedience to divine law was the very essence of religion. Atonement implied that, since Christ died for all, men were universally salvageable. The sacraments were the means of grace for appropriating the *aid* of Christ's merits. In his home, therefore, Wesley was taught to think in terms of godliness of works, devout striving for the good life and breaking of self-will with the help of a mystical awareness of God.[3] Rules for personal conduct and Churchly allegiance were both specific and important. A life of pious discipline was essential to finding God's favor.

Upon leaving home for further schooling at Charterhouse, John

---

[2] The biographical material is based on sundry sources, notably John Wesley's *Journal*; J. H. Overton, *John Wesley*; Oscar Sherwin, *John Wesley, Friend of the People*; Francis McConnell, *John Wesley*; Gerald Kennedy, *Heritage and Destiny*.

[3] Cf. William R. Cannon, *The Theology of John Wesley*, Chapter 2.

became a bit lax in his piety for a time, while remaining quite con-
scientious in doctrine. At Oxford, not negatively influenced in an
intellectual sense either by the increasing empiricism or by the religious skepticism of the time, he turned to the reading of certain
religious books of growing recognition. This was about the time he
entered Lincoln College. He read Jeremy Taylor's *Rules and Exercises of Holy Living and Dying,* Thomas a Kempis's devotional
classic *The Imitation of Christ,* and William Law's *Christian Perfection* and *A Serious Call to a Devout Life.* He took them seriously,
and each of them stressed the devout life of self-abnegation and
striving, thus confirming his basic views, held since boyhood, and
bolstering his new resolve to lead a life of disciplined devotion,
something then understood to be the basic essential of Christian
salvation.[4] When he was twenty-two the young Mr. Wesley began to
sense that "true religion was seated in the heart," while extending
to all activity. This was while he was under the influence of Thomas
a Kempis's writing and the constraints of his father to enter holy
orders.[5]

Contrary to Piette, a Roman Catholic interpreter,[6] the reading
of the devotional classics of Taylor, a Kempis and Law did not add
up to Wesley's conversion, or the great turning point in his life.
Though they influenced his devotional resolve, they did not make a
major change in his thinking so much as they enhanced what he
already believed. What is more, these devotional works did nothing,
we contend, to mitigate Wesley's inner anxiety. He even felt that
a Kempis was "too strict," though challenging. Much the same applies to his reading of William Law's works. Whatever specific influences they had, Wesley continued to interpret religion as a matter
of legalistic striving.[7] This only intensified his anxiety.

Specifically, Jeremy Taylor's *Rules and Exercises for Holy Living
and Dying* did nothing to alleviate the young Mr. Wesley's deep-
seated fear of death, a fear that remained with him until Aldersgate.

---

[4] Wesley's *Journal,* entries and comments for May 24, 1738, in which he
reviews his spiritual sojourn since the age of ten, pp. 465 f.

[5] *Ibid.,* p. 466.

[6] M. Piette, *John Wesley in the Evolution of Protestantism,* tr. J. B.
Howard (Sheed and Ward, 1937).

[7] *Journal,* p. 467.

Wesley writes of those years as a student: "Yet when, after continuing some years in course, I apprehended myself to be near death, I could not find that all this gave me any comfort or any assurance of acceptance with God." This must not be overlooked. "I dragged on heavily," he went on, "finding no comfort or help therein . . ."[8] Of a later time he wrote: "In my return to England, January, 1738, being in imminent danger of death, and very uneasy on that account, I was strongly convinced that the cause of that uneasiness was unbelief; and that the gaining a true, living faith was the 'one thing needful' for me."[9]

Thus we see how Wesley's earlier piety was a sincere, but self-centered striving that yielded little peace. The devotional classics proved to be as much misleading as leading, since they only helped intensify his inner struggle. Retrospectively, he writes of this period: "I had been all this time building on the sand . . ." referring to it as a carnal state of bondage in seeking "to establish my own righteousness."[10] This perspective remained with Wesley while doing missionary work in Georgia, but with pronounced misgivings, as we shall see. "Before," writes Wesley of his period of devotional resolve, "I had willingly served sin; now it was unwillingly; but I still served it." This is a truly heart-searching admission.

On the other hand, the devotional writings left an indelible impression on him. Their strong ethical emphases stayed with him even in his post-Aldersgate theology, which met with a pronounced reorientation in that hour. But why did these devotional works fail to guide Wesley into the freedom of soul for which he yearned? Basically, because they intensified his guilt and fear, especially upon

---

8 *Ibid.*, pp. 467, 470 f. Maximin Piette, in Book III, Chapter 6, pp. 305 ff., thinks Wesley's "conversion" should be placed fourteen years earlier, in 1725, the year he was ordained deacon and about the time he was taking the work of Bishop Jeremy Taylor seriously. Cf. the discussions on Wesley's youth at Charterhouse, Chapter II, pp. 231 ff., and Wesley's university days, when he read a Kempis, Taylor and Law, pp. 238 f., 248 f., 259 f. Piette attacks Luke Tyerman for describing the youthful Wesley prior to Aldersgate as a "great sinner," who had made "shipwreck" of his life, p. 232. The Roman Catholic interpreter of Wesley may have a case in point but he does not address himself to the real issues at stake such as we contend for in this chapter.

9 *Ibid.*, pp. 468, 470.

10 *Ibid.*, p. 470.

demanding mature fruits of righteousness without clarifying the
Word-grounded, grace-given root of salvation by faith. "I was still
'under the law,' not 'under grace,'" says Wesley of his days in
Savannah.[11] This is exceedingly important to understand, if we are
to do justice either to Wesley's spiritual experience or his theological
regrounding therein.

Thus from 1720 to 1738 the religion Wesley held to was basically
that of his childhood, a matter of pious self-discipline. Though he
looked to mysticism for a time, he gave it up about the time he joined
the Holy Club at Oxford. In 1735, when Wesley went to Georgia
as a missionary, he was prompted largely by the desire to do good
to prove he was good.[12] All this time he reflected a lack of understanding of the grace of God basic to reconciliation. Or, if he understood it with his head, he did not with his heart. It was not something
existentially relevant to him. Faith was still a pursuit and a struggle
to attain holiness through obedience to law. The inner peace, assurance, and free-flowing love of God for which he yearned were not
real to his soul. Religion was more bondage than liberty; not that he
saw it as bondage, but he did not know it as liberty.

But the day of liberation did come to Wesley. A great contrast
is to be seen in his outlook before and after Aldersgate. Four months
after his return to England from Georgia, he was still inwardly uneasy and even tempted to give up. The Moravian student, Peter
Böhler, suggested that he preach faith until he had it. This was
encouraging. When he reluctantly accepted the invitation to attend
a meeting in London, on the evening of Wednesday, May 24, 1738,
the climactic moment came. Of this he wrote in his *Journal:*

> In the evening I went very unwillingly to a society in Aldersgate
> Street, where one was reading Luther's Preface to the Epistle to the
> Romans. About a quarter before nine, while he was describing the
> change which God works in the heart through faith in Christ, I felt
> my heart strangely warmed. I felt I did trust in Christ, Christ alone
> for salvation; and an assurance was given me that he had taken
> away my sins, even *mine,* and saved *me* from the law of sin and
> death.

11 *Ibid.*
12 Cannon, *op. cit.*

Here is the turning point in Wesley's life—and the watershed in his theological understanding. Prior to this time of illumination by the Word and liberation in his soul, Wesley's theology was bound to a legalistic view, and his life was lived accordingly. A holy striving was deemed the means to divine favor. After Aldersgate, however, his outlook was different. Not egocentric, it became Christocentric, as a fresh orientation in the doctrine of justification by faith was seen existentially relevant to his life. His theology was affected profoundly, because he himself was. Yet he was affected because his theology was! True, his theology may have remained sterile, without the significance of the "warmed heart," but let it not be overlooked that without a theological vivification of existential pertinence to Wesley in that hour, Aldersgate would not have been Aldersgate, as we think of it, neither the Aldersgate of the warmed heart nor of fresh beginnings in life and thought.

Wesley himself has expressed it perfectly: before Aldersgate he was "more like a servant"; after Aldersgate he was "more like a son."[13] Here was the "true, living faith" for which he had yearned. Here was a trustful self-commitment to the Living Word who encountered him in that hour. Not basic but symptomatic was the "heart strangely warmed," the subjective side of his assurance by faith, the inner aspect of the Word of Christ existentially relevant in that moment of encounter. Basic to that moment was a facet of the revealed Word of God not previously understood with such personal meaningfulness. This is not to depreciate one iota of Wesley's "heart warming," rather it is to clarify its basic reference: faith in Christ. A vivid experience *per se* is not enough to account for the great transition either in Wesley's life or in his ministry. Central is not the experience as such but the Word of Life that evoked it. If we may characterize it in another way, Aldersgate was Wesley's Kierkegaardian Moment, that instant of eternal dimension when he saw himself confronted by the divine Absolute on its own terms. On the brink of despair, to be enlarged below, Wesley saw now his need of what Kierkegaard called later an "absolute relation to the Absolute." And who is equal to that save by the grace of God? Hitherto Wesley had been misdirected, only to settle for his finite

[13] Wesley's *Journal*, Jan. 29, 1738, p. 423.

pursuits and emulations of the infinite. Now he saw in whom he really had faith.

Salvation was seen differently after Aldersgate. No longer a product of devout works of righteousness, to which divine grace was little more than a supplementary aid, it now meant a new relation and restored condition. Such a faith relation was a divine gift; hence thereafter Wesley could preach "the free grace of God," making possible the justified status essential to the true Christian perspective. What Wesley came to see existentially as centered in the doctrine of justification by faith, he came to see doctrinally as the focal point of his theology and message. Not his only theme, it became, however, the foundation stone of his theology. Thus, for Wesley, a doctrinal vivification yielded a personal awakening, which gave rise to a theological reorientation of far-reaching significance. Aldersgate would not have become so efficacious to Wesley's ministry were it not for the new understanding of grace that came to him. Word-centered, it was not another religious experience; it was an encounter with the Living Christ. "And I felt I did trust in *Christ*," he said, ". . . that he had taken away *my* sins, even *mine*, and saved *me* from the law of sin and death." For the first time in his life Wesley saw the meaning of the saving Word in the *hic et nunc* of faith. He was embraced now by Him who is "our eternal contemporary." A faith not merely *credo* and *ergo* but *pistis;* not merely assent and work, it was a trustful relation, a total self-commitment, It was this new faith perspective and relation that yielded both the warmed heart and the revamped theology. As the Word and Spirit possessed him in his moment of "heart warming," Wesley not only represented "a brand plucked from the fire" but a personification of the *fire in the brand.*

Existentially, there were several factors contributing to the collapse of Wesley's earlier view of Christian salvation, factors both personal and theological in connotation. Among them was his profound sense of failure upon leaving Georgia, intensified by an embarrassing experience not long before he left. We are not saying here that Wesley had failed objectively, but that he failed existentially, that he had failed in not finding his true selfhood, in not fulfilling his basic purpose as well as in not finding the inner peace he desired.[14] "I went to Georgia to help convert the Indians," he wrote in his *Journal*, "but oh! who shall convert me?"[15] What is this self-appraisal but a form of deep-seated despair and penitent and sorrowful misgiving about the divine meaning of his very existence. More than a rhetorical expression, it reflected the dark night of the despairing soul at the brink of a redeeming dawn.

Wesley's sense of spiritual deficiency had deepened even two years earlier, when aboard ship, on the journey to Georgia, he witnessed the composure of his Moravian friends, who could sing God's praise in the midst of stormy seas. Wesley desired just such an assurance in the face of death but he could not claim it. His existential anxiety obsessed him. Now upon returning home he was haunted by that same deep-seated dread. Later, he refers to it as "the fear of the sea, which I had both dreaded and abhorred from my youth."[16] At the same time Wesley gradually sensed that his piety was not necessarily the center of his salvation. Furthermore, his experience with the American Indians had convinced him that human nature, even that of the aborigines, was not as "good" as he had assumed nor as readily susceptible to the Gospel as he had anticipated.[17] All this contributed to the Aldersgate moment, for it contributed to Wesley's preliminary anxiety, uncertainty, and spiritual despair.

Before moving on we might ask: Was the Georgia mission the failure that Wesley seems to have felt it was at the moment when he wrote those words in his *Journal?* Not objectively, we repeat. George Whitefield is known to have said of Wesley's work in Georgia, "The good Mr. John Wesley has done in America is inexpressible. . . . Oh, that I may follow him as he followed Christ."[18] Surely Wesley's ministry in Georgia was far from barren, then; but that is still not the basic issue. The real issue is whether John Wesley understood faithwise within his heart, within his own concrete selfhood, the peace of divine grace that the Gospel proffers men. His own inner

---

[14] Cannon fails to drive home this important distinction, which shall be enlarged below.

[15] Wesley's *Journal*, Jan. 24, 1738, p. 418.

[16] *Ibid.*, Feb. 3, 1738. The Wesley hymns often allude to the storms and seas of life. Cf. notations for Jan. 1738, pp. 417 f.

[17] *Ibid.*, July 9, 1737, p. 367. Cf. Overton, *John Wesley*, p. 50 ff.

[18] Cited by Overton, *op. cit.*, p. 53.

existence, as he alone knew it, was still befuddled. Even so, God
had honored his objective witness to the Word.

Wesley originally went to Georgia to evangelize the Indians. The
natives under Chief Tomo-chachi had been disappointed by the
Spaniards, who baptized without giving instruction. The Indians wel-
comed Wesley, but shortly afterward another priest's withdrawal
led to Wesley's being diverted to regular parish work. It was then
that he met with some resistance from people not congenial to his
high-churchly ways. This also contributed to his inner uneasiness.
Further contacts with the Moravians who had settled in Georgia
continued to make him dissatisfied with his own spiritual status. He
did not seem to have what they had. This appears to have been intensified by an embarrassing experience just before his departure
from Georgia.[19] Mr. Williamson, a man not very close to the Church,
took Wesley to court for not administering communion to his wife,
the former Sophia Hopkey, to whom Wesley himself had once been
engaged, and who had neglected her Church duties. Doubtless this
experience was most taxing and intensified Wesley's sense of failure
and misgiving.

It was aboard ship while returning to England that Wesley wrote
those words of profound despair and yearning: ". . . but oh! who
shall convert me?" Whereupon he added these lines of self-examination: "I have a fair summer religion. I can talk well, but let death
look me in the face, and my spirit is troubled. Alienated as I am from
the life of God, I am a child of wrath, an heir of hell."[20] Not simply
words of self-condemnation, these are the words of a man who
lacked the peace of a right relationship to God on God's terms. His
disciplined piety and self-sacrifice, admirable as they were objectively, had not given him peace existentially. He did not know the
personal relevance of a justifying grace. Existentially, he was steeped
in a dread of death and a lack of accord with God.

True, some years later Wesley himself said of the above-cited
comment in his *Journal:* "I am not sure of this."[21] But he looked

---

[19] Wesley's *Journal*, Feb. to Aug., 1737, pp. 318–88.

[20] *Ibid.*, Jan. 24, 1738, p. 418.

[21] *Ibid.*, Jan. 29, p. 422. Footnote comment.

back at that hour of his life from a different vantage point, a perspective too historical and aloof to do the earlier experience full justice. Even so, it was then that Wesley said retrospectively: "I had even the faith of a servant, though not of a son."[22] Does not this express the matter with acuity? When Wesley was returning to England by sea, surely he had a measure of some kind of faith in God and was not literally "alienated from God," but it was that of a misdirected, legalistic piety; indeed, the faith of a "servant," not a "son." It was just such legalistic piety, we must understand, that had *failed* Wesley. This failure was what haunted his mind when he wrote: ". . . who shall convert me?" Aboard ship again, he knew he lacked something basic, especially in the face of death. And what is the fear of death but one of the elemental frustrations that only a justifying faith can efface? Wesley wanted the peace and poise that the Moravians had claimed and demonstrated, and that he lacked. In short, he was afraid of death as they were not, and this implied that he was not ready to meet his God, because he was not right with God.

A significant reflection of Wesley's deficient faith prior to Aldersgate is epitomized in a conversation with the Moravian leader Spangenberg, whom he met upon arriving in Savannah. Said Spangenberg: "Do you know Jesus Christ?" Wesley could only reply: "I know he is the Savior of the world." "True," said Spangenberg, "but do you know he has saved *you?*" This was the point at issue that Wesley had not yet come to understand existentially; he lacked the joy and peace of a conscious salvation.

As already intimated, the joyous witness and composure of the Moravians left a profound impression upon Wesley's mind, as did their doctrine of the witness of the Spirit, to which they introduced him in Georgia. There can be little doubt that Wesley desired to know what they knew. Honest with himself, he wrote in his *Journal* that he was "in want of the faith whereby alone we are saved."[23] This yearning reflects, just a few weeks before Aldersgate, nothing less than his inability at this time to appreciate subjectively, existentially,

---

[22] *Ibid.*, footnote comment, p. 422. Cf. Overton, *op. cit.*, pp. 57 f.
[23] *Journal*, March 4, 1738.

the very meaning of justification by faith. But the Moravians helped him to think and seek God in a new way. This became the positive side of what was preliminary to Aldersgate.

Back at Oxford, Wesley met Peter Böhler, a younger Moravian student who had just come over from Germany. In their conversations, Böhler told Wesley not to give up, as he was tempted to do, but to preach faith until he had it. Wesley respected this counsel and carried on with this encouragement. Yet in subsequent discussions with Böhler, he expressed doubt concerning a saving faith that could be acquired in a moment. Böhler's testimony concerning this and the witness of the Spirit made Wesley turn to his New Testament as well as to several living witnesses. He stopped debating, and cried out: "Lord, help Thou my unbelief!" Three weeks before Aldersgate, on May 1, 1738, when Wesley began to understand Peter Böhler's witness to a justifying faith, he turned to his old teacher, William Law, expressing disappointment for his failure to clarify this faith. The correspondence unfortunately led to a theological estrangement of a sort, though Wesley continued to speak highly of Law, and Law never wrote anything against Wesley.[24]

At Aldersgate, in a simple meeting place, Wesley came to see the Christ-centered simplicity of faith. As Luther's *Commentary* on the Epistle to the Romans was read that evening of the twenty-fourth of May, in 1738, Wesley saw more clearly than ever before what faith really meant. "I felt I did trust in Christ," he wrote in his *Journal*, "and that he had taken away my sins, even mine, and saved me from the law of sin and death." What a contrast from the entry two months before! A justifying grace understood by faith now became the center of Wesley's life, rather than a devout but self-centered striving. Grace superseded all meritorious devotion based on moralistic and legalistic pursuit. Understanding this was a far cry from the perspective of a missionary set on proving his righteousness. Thus the Pauline doctrines of "justification by faith" and "spiritual adoption" gave new life to Wesley's soul, together with "the witness of the Spirit" interpreted in terms of the warmed heart. It was this fresh awakening to the meaning of faith that became essential to Wesley's theological reorientation, we contend, and that vitally in-

---

[24] Overton, *op. cit.*, pp. 61 ff.

spired the rest of his ministry and put his theology into new focus.

For Wesley, Aldersgate vivified the meaning of divine grace, not only experientially, but theologically as well. This we would emphasize. So great was the shift in Wesley's thinking that he came to realize that even good works, apart from God's reconciliation to man, are spiritually void and perverted by mixed motives. Thus grace was now seen to be no mere supplement to one's devotion, but an indispensable necessity, without which all devotion is askew. How does this contrast stand out in Wesley's life?

A week after Aldersgate Wesley attended a meeting at the home of a new friend, John Hutton. During the reading of a sermon by Bishop Blackall, he stood up to declare, to everyone's amazement, that he had not been a Christian until the past week. This may seem somewhat disturbing, as it was to the Huttons and others at that meeting, but to reiterate the issue, we must seek to understand Wesley's assertion existentially, not objectively. He stated: "When we renounce everything but faith and get into Christ, then, and not till then, have we any reason to believe that we are Christians."[25] John Wesley's Anglican friends, including his brother Samuel, could not understand this assertion, in view of the covenant and grace implied by the sacraments. But no one, either then or now, can understand it, save as each sees things as John Wesley saw them, that is, from within himself, as he increasingly came to a spiritual despair that was the brink of his existential encounter with the saving and meaning-giving Word of Life.

All this and more must be brought to bear upon John Wesley's Aldersgate experience, with not only its experiental implications but its theological relevance and clarification. What vividly affected Wesley's faith perspective profoundly affected his entire theology. This is what we mean by the existential context of Wesley's theology, a matter interpreters of Wesley need to see more clearly today. This is to say that a doctrinal distinction contributed both to Wesley's Aldersgate experience and proved fundamental to the refurbishing of his theological position.

Thus Aldersgate was indeed an important turning point. To minimize it is not to have heeded Wesley's own appraisal of it, not

---

[25] *Journal, op. cit.,* p. 480. Cf. Overton, *op. cit.,* p. 64.

to have taken seriously, for instance, his outstanding sermon "The Almost Christian," based on Acts 26:28. In this powerful sermon, preached at Oxford in July, 1741, Wesley expounds the difference between being an *almost* Christian and being *altogether* a Christian. After describing the "almost Christian" as a person who is in all appearances religious in his endeavors and practices, Wesley becomes personal, stating:

> I did thus far for many years, as many of this place can testify: Using diligence to eschew all evil, and to have a conscience void of offense: redeeming the time, buying up every opportunity to do good to all men; constantly and carefully using all the public and all the private means of grace; endeavoring after a steady seriousness of behavior, at all times and in all places: And God is my record, before whom I stand, doing all this in sincerity; having a real design to serve God, a hearty desire to do his will in all things, to please him who had called me to fight the good fight, and to lay hold of eternal life. Yet my own conscience beareth me witness in the Holy Ghost, that all this time I was but *almost a Christian.*[26]

What, then, was the big difference Aldersgate represented for Wesley, before and after? Certainly not a sudden resurgence of concern for the devout life. If anyone was devout and devoted, Wesley was. Rather, it was a new perspective and motivation based on an important scriptural teaching. As Martin Luther's *Commentary* to the Epistle to the Romans was read, Wesley saw clearly for the first time the personal pertinence of the doctrine of justification by faith as enunciated by Saint Paul. What Luther had found revolutionary in his life and thought, Wesley had come to know in his. Thus in that moment of encounter with the Word he sensed his present acceptability to God solely on God's terms, not his own. He saw, too, that the "altogether Christian" now could love God and his neighbor from a new Christ-centered standpoint and with a new motive. Such a fresh motivation was not of self but of grace, not for merit but in trust, a direct personal commitment and relation to God on terms of an undeserving grace.

Noteworthy is the fact that when Wesley, in that Aldersgate moment, could by divine grace "accept himself because he was accepted," to adapt a contemporary expression from Paul Tillich, his

---

[26] John Wesley, *Sermons on Several Occasions*, Vol. I, (1794), p. 35.

freedom of soul immediately burst forth with prayerful expressions of love, even for persons who had abused him.[27] Thus a new relationship with God opened up new relationships with his fellow men. The Gospel of grace and atoning love as centered in the cross became now the very focal point of Wesley's life and thought, whereas prior to Aldersgate they were from secondary to peripheral. A justified status gave new meaning and motivation to his life as the love of God flooded his heart. Christocentric rather than egocentric, religion now meant a "faith that worketh by love." As a vital personal and trustful relation to God was opened up for Wesley, the sanctified life he had sought was given both a foundation and a possibility that he had not seen before. Wesley saw the new life of love anchored, as he put it, in "a sure trust and confidence which a man hath in God, that by the merits of Christ his sins *are* forgiven, and he reconciled to the favour of God—whereof doth follow a loving heart, to obey his commandments."[28] Thus it is important to see here how justification by faith was seen by Wesley to be the basic condition of a righteousness of loving and free obedience. It gave a new outlook to all of life, for from that time on God's grace had a priority that gave a new dimension to all of Wesley's individual endeavors.

At Aldersgate Wesley came to see that God must first do something for a man that he cannot do for himself, and this before man can do anything truly pleasing, significant, and loving for God. Only a liberated soul can know the liberty of grace. Thus, we reiterate, Wesley's entire ministry, his preaching, and his evangelistic endeavors were given positive theological reorientation at Aldersgate. Justification was now seen to be the only condition of reconciliation, and the true door to sanctification. As Wesley himself said, the true faith-relation meant "being justified freely by his grace, through the redemption that is in Jesus: Knowing we have peace with God through Jesus Christ; Rejoicing in hope of the glory of God, and having the love of God shed abroad in our heart, by the Holy Ghost given unto us;"[29] Such a new-found faith was bound to affect Wesley's entire theology and his subsequent preaching.

At Aldersgate Wesley recovered both for himself and for his

27 Wesley's *Journal*, pp. 422, 476 f. Cf. Paul Tillich, *The Courage to Be.*
28 Wesley, *Sermons*, Vol. I, p. 38.
29 *Ibid.*, p. 41.

generation a biblical and redemptive theology meaningful to men just as they are, while pointing them also to what they could become in Christ. Not new, it was a recovery of New Testament doctrine based on the message that men need to *be* saved and to have a Savior. Men, however sinful, can be restored to God now. Thus Aldersgate meant that a frantic and fatiguing piety of legalistic striving was to be displaced by a peace-giving trust.

Not so much his "conversion" (Wesley later saw that the term was frequently misleading), it was, nevertheless, a revelation for Wesley, or, better, an existential realization of what the revelation of God in Christ really means. Not a turning away from a radically sinful existence, here was, nevertheless, a new lease on life through the freedom and peace that accompanies the realization of sonship, not only by creation, but by redemption through grace. Bishop Francis Gerald Ensley has well stated of Wesley's pre-Aldersgate problem: "His plight was not that of the Prodigal, penitently throwing himself on the Father's mercy. It was more that of the prissy Elder Brother, who had been slaving unhappily in the Father's house without feeling the privileges of his love."[30] What to Wesley had been a load before Aldersgate now became a lift! What had seemed his ruin was now his release. What had been his despair had now become his delight.

Not only was Aldersgate a turning point experientially, but also theologically. And this in the fullest sense, both doctrinally and ethically. Ethically speaking, Wesley's existential encounter with the saving Word had both personal and social implications. His heart-warming experience was such that immediately he burst forth with loving prayers for those who had abused him in the past.[31] Here we see how a fresh Christ-centered faith inspired in Wesley a loving concern for others; it gave a new incentive and dynamic to all of life. While good works are now understood differently, they are still embraced as an important aspect of a holiness of new affections and expressed righteousness.

This is important, theologically speaking, for Wesley did not substitute justification for holiness, but saw justification undergirding life unto true holiness. It was precisely for this reason that Wesley found it necessary to break with his Moravian friends less than three

[30] F. Gerald Ensley, *John Wesley, Evangelist,* p. 14.
[31] Wesley's *Journal,* May 24, 1738 (14), p. 476.

years after the Aldersgate experience. He saw among them too little regard for an actuated sanctification of life, or a justification that opened the door to holy living.[32] It is in this respect that the writings of Taylor, Law and a Kempis still left an indelible imprint on Wesley's theology, while their appeals to devout living are now seen in the light of the primacy of faith in a justifying grace.

The Christian social implications of Wesley's new-found ethics, based on his theological reorientation at Aldersgate, is also exceedingly important. This must not be overlooked. At the time, there was a manual being used in close association with the Church of England's prayerbook. It was entitled *The Whole Duty of Man*. An underlying theme of the manual was that class distinctions were divinely ordained and a person's betters or superiors were to be reverenced. Noteworthy is the fact that prior to his Aldersgate experience Wesley regarded this work highly, but after receiving his new outlook on the Christian life he regarded it as "a pedantic, hypocritical heap of rubbish which nullified the Brotherhood of Man."[33] Just as race prejudice is an acute social issue in our day, social classism was one in Wesley's day. Many a dignitary, including the Countess of Huntingdon, expressed disfavor with the Wesleyan movement's tendency to make all men equal before God. Thus we see how Wesley's theological awakening at Aldersgate had far-reaching effects, even making his evangelism a powerful social influence throughout Great Britain. Laboring men who had lost respect for the Church and the clergy were now reclaimed for Christ and the Kingdom. Let it be said that what Wesley discovered existentially at Aldersgate was not only of personal significance but of ethical and social influence as well. And how could this be, save that a doctrinal truth had come alive for him with such meaning that his entire theology was put into a new and proper focus.

Since the existential context of Wesley's theology is at the forefront of our attention, it is important that we briefly relate it to his thought in general. As much as Wesley differed with the Calvinists over the question of election, for instance, he appreciated both their emphasis upon the primacy of grace and their place for faith as

---

[32] John Wesley specifies this in a letter to his brother Charles, April 22, 1741. *Letters of John Wesley*, edited by Eayres, p. 74.

[33] Cf. Sherwin, *op. cit.*, p. 26.

Christian experience. In short, he did not yield evangelical principles merely because he could not accept predestination. To consider
Wesley's ardent summoning back of the Church from a moralistic
religion and the worship of humanistic notions to the worship of the
true and saving God in Christ is to recognize much in common with
the Reformation, on the one hand, and the emphasis of the neo-Reformation theology of today, on the other. It is a commentary in itself that Wesley's Aldersgate renewal in both faith and doctrine was
linked with a reconsideration of Luther's expression of Paul's teachings.

In some respects, Wesley's empirical appeal anticipated the emphasis of Friedrich Schleiermacher, seventy-five years later. Both
stood for a subjectively vivid religious experience; however, Schleiermacher's immanental system was more apt to foster the idea of
religion as "natural" rather than "graceful," as witnessed by his
monistic theological structure.[34] After Aldersgate Wesley laid a more
pronounced emphasis upon the doctrine of "the witness of the Holy
Spirit." Though based on the message of the Word, the witness was
as much subjective as objective. It meant the Spirit of God attested
by the spirit of the believer. Schleiermacher, however, held to a more
ready-made "feeling" of the Spirit, something quite natural to men.
At Aldersgate the subjective element may be seen to rest upon the
objective, for when Wesley refers to what he feels of trust and forgiveness, it centers dependently upon the revealed Word of God's
grace and what he has wrought in the atoning deed of Christ. In this
respect, Wesley's religious empiricism is much closer to being existential than Schleiermacher's, for Wesley both in his faith experience
and his preaching vivifies the individual's dependence, not merely
upon his religious feelings, but upon Christ as the redemptive Word
addressing him from beyond himself.

Through Wesley "Christian experience" became practically a new
term in eighteenth-century theology. Scripture and experience were
both considered basic while not antithetical. "It is safe to say," re-
marks George Cell, "that no other teacher of the Christian Church
and preacher of the Gospel ever laid upon experience so heavy a
burden of responsibility for discerning and confirming the truth
values of the Christian faith . . . Wesley brought the whole Christian

---

[34] F. Schleiermacher, *The Christian Faith* and *Addresses on Religion.*

world back to religion and experience; in religion experience and reality come to the same thing."[35] Cell also states:

> Moreover, it was not the Moravians, as commonly supposed, but Wesley who first insisted when the truth-values in the doctrine of Justification by faith were being put to the test, and after having been strongly urged upon his acceptance by the Moravians, that the argument from the plain teaching of the New Testament could not alone carry the conclusion with it but must first be vouched for by the argument from Christian experience.[36]

Even so, too much emphasis can be placed upon experience in regard to Wesley's theology. While seeing the strong place of spiritual assurance as highly pertinent to the individual believer, Wesley eventually became sensitive to the abuses to which the appeal to experience might lend itself. Aware of how the idea of "conversion" can be interpreted in overly restrictive terms, he also realized that an overly subjective view of "assurance" is apt to be made a substitute for the Word and the true doctrine of grace.[37]

A reaction against extreme mysticism is centered in Wesley's emphasis upon a God-given faith. Feelings, good works, or natural reason, when pondered as in mysticism, are insufficient and antithetical to this God-given faith. Mystics are apt to dissociate themselves from the fellowship of believers in Christ and the means of grace, and claim that when man enters a passive state he is *one* with God. This, of course, Wesley could not hold to; it was the difference between "a religious hermit" and "a Christian frontiersman." Wesley attacks some mysticism, however, as being more of a dependence upon the Church than upon God. He consistently maintained: "The Gate of Religion is faith and the Word of God in the Scriptures." He even said that a Christian "called to perfection" should neither "neglect nor rest in the means of grace," which is the hearing and reading of the Word, prayer, sacrament, the witness and fellowship of faith. Thus the subject or recipient of grace is neither to be self-sufficient in any way nor utterly inert or passive, but active, not only to enjoy grace, but to reflect and spread the Gospel as a social, not just a solitary, religion.[38]

[35] George Cell, *The Rediscovery of John Wesley,* pp. 47 f, Cf. pp. 64, 72 f.
[36] *Ibid.,* p. 84.
[37] *Ibid.,* p. 152.
[38] Cell, *op. cit.,* pp. 96–153.

The doctrinal and experiential consequence of Aldersgate was that Wesley now could help men see what God could do *for* and *to* them, whereby he might do things *in* and *through* them as well. Redemption, then, as related to personal experience could now make for changes of far-reaching proportions—and it did! The new relation with God wrought for men new relations both with themselves and with all others in their lives. The result was an evangelical faith of revolutionary relevance, a faith-experience grounded in the Word of God as highly applicable to all areas of human existence.

It is our contention that just as Wesley's personal life gained the new birth of freedom through a clarification of New Testament doctrine, so his entire ministry gained foundational support and articulation from his theological readjustment, which began at Aldersgate. Aldersgate, therefore, represents profoundly the existential context of Wesley's theology. The vivid faith experience was not an end in itself, but meant, rather, a new focal point for both his personal life and his evangelistic endeavors, as a redemptive and theological renewal came into his life. Thus, in a sense, Wesley's Aldersgate experience was existentially renewed day by day in the light of the same Word that illuminated his soul, a "quarter before nine" that evening in May, 1738.

Wesley's preaching was given now a theological undergirding of marked significance. As he preached and wrote, his message became more and more that of a coherent Christ-centered theology, one seeking to reflect the fullest meaning of the gospel of redemption. His theology became, thereupon, one that was highly relevant to both sinner and saint. To the sinner it offered the maximum hope; to the saint it offered the maximum challenge, responsibility, maturity and vision. One without the other becomes an imbalanced, if not immature, theology, as Wesley came to see. Thus Aldersgate was a spiritual renewal for Wesley, because it was a doctrinal clarification of pronounced existential pertinence. This, in turn, gave rise to a revitalized, freshly illuminated theology that was essential to Wesley's most effective work. Indeed, Wesley proved to be "a brand plucked from the fire," but only because of the "fire in the brand."

CHAPTER V

THE DIALECTICAL CREATIVITY OF WESLEY'S THEOLOGY

THE eighteenth century was a period of crisis for Western Christendom. The rising tides of humanism and rationalism released with the Enlightenment were taking their toll, while a prevalent deism was helping to reduce Christianity to little more than a moralistic religion. This was especially the case in the British Isles, and it was beginning to be felt even on the eastern shores of America.

An older Protestantism of scholastic form was dwindling as a newer type of a manward reference was gaining momentum, seemingly to sever itself from its true fountainhead in the Reformation and a subsequent orthodoxy affixed to firm creeds. As the sciences found their stride, the appeal to the empirical method increased the challenge to religious authority in whatever form, scriptural or ecclesiastical. A new approach was desperately needed, if evangelical Protestantism was to continue to be a creative force and withstand the onslaught of the prevalent deism and humanism of the age.

Providentially, a man appeared on the scene to help bring about the new approach to New Testament Christianity. In so doing, John Wesley was theologically a major bridge between the old and the new Protestantism. Grounded in the classical theologies but aware of contemporary trends and needs, Wesley became the mastermind witness of the Evangelical Awakening that shook the British Isles into a new consciousness of God. In some respects, Wesley epitomized the religious conflicts of the previous two centuries, but only as he came to grips with basic issues and looked afresh to the New Testament for answers relevant to men of his day.

Similarly, it can be said that Wesley anticipated some of the religious conflicts of the next two centuries, for some of his basic appeals set important precedents for reappraisals in Christian theology.

This was largely due to his bipolar emphasis upon the indispensable grace of God, on the one hand, and the responsible role of man, on the other. Nineteenth-century theology saw recoveries in the role of man; twentieth-century theology has seen afresh the primacy of divine grace. It may be said that today men need to see again the bipolar relation of the two, so as to minimize the importance of neither. In this respect, a fresh look at the theology of John Wesley can be enlightening stimulus to further creative thought in contemporary theology.

Wesley was not a specialized, systematic theologian as had been earlier Protestant leaders like Calvin and Melancthon; nevertheless, his theology, far from slipshod, was truly systematic, creative and constructive. Too many outside the Wesleyan tradition, as well as within, have not become familiar with this fact. Wesley found it necessary to defend his convictions, and when he preached his discourses became strong dialectical arguments communicable and persuasive because of their dynamic yet logical structure. "The Almost Christian" is a sermon that serves as a good case in point.[1]

It is no exaggeration to say that John Wesley became the most influential Christian leader since the Reformation of the sixteenth century. His one purpose was to preach salvation by faith in Christ and to "spread scriptural holiness throughout the land." Carefully understood, it can be said that as bridge and bridge builder between the older and newer Protestantisms, Wesley was "both the fulfiller and conqueror of the humanistic religion of the Enlightenment."[2] This, we maintain, is because of his dynamic bipolar position. Not confident in man, he was nevertheless confident in redeemed man! Christ was for him the big difference for both soul and society.

If we are to appreciate Wesley's theological, bridge-building function within Christian history, we must see him both as a man of his time and as a Christian conscious of what he owed both to Reformation theology and what preceded as well as followed it. With the New Testament as his foundation, Wesley thought creatively through the issues posed by the major strands of interpretation to appear in his-

---

[1] John Wesley, *Sermons on Several Occasions*, Vol. I (1794).
[2] George C. Cell, *The Rediscovery of John Wesley*, p. 4.

tory. One cannot be conversant with his theology without seeing the marks, direct and indirect, of the thinking of such varied leaders as Luther and Calvin, Thomas Aquinas, Augustine, the great mystics and pietists, including Jeremy Taylor, Thomas a Kempis and William Law. This, despite the fact that one cannot completely identify Wesley's mature thinking with any single one of them.

Less than three decades ago George Cell reappraised Wesley's work and theology as resting firmly on the foundations laid by Luther and Calvin, and that this made him the liaison between medieval and modern Christianity.[3] There is a strong sense in which this is true, but the writer must agree with William R. Cannon that Cell's case is somewhat overstated.[4] Though Wesley's basic soteriology, as centered about the doctrines of sin and justification by faith, has much in common with the Reformers, an identification exceedingly important to remember, it must not be overlooked that Wesley provides a more active, responsible and hopeful side to his soteriology, as anchored in his doctrine of sanctification. In fact, in this respect Wesley has more in common with the pattern, though not the system, of the Thomists, since he integrates an activated righteousness of good works with the new outlook and Spirit-qualified faith of the justified believer.

With much in common with Puritan piety, Wesley pushes further the implications of John Calvin, who would say to his people: "Make your calling and election sure," that is, live out your Christ-centered faith and show what grace means to you. Both Calvin and Wesley believed that a life of actuated righteousness was indicative of the work of grace. Wesley simply saw greater possibilities for this life through the sanctifying work of the Holy Spirit. Then, too, the place Wesley makes for the inner assurance of salvation is more in keeping with the mystics, pietists and religious empiricists than with Luther, though Calvin also has a strong place for this assurance.

One does not do full justice to Wesley's theology until one sees how Wesley both appreciated and qualified the more classical Protestant theology as well as challenged and corrected the moralistic

---

3 *Ibid.,* p. 5. This is one of Cell's basic claims.
4 William R. Cannon, *The Theology of John Wesley,* pp. 105 f.

trends within a contemporary Anglicanism influenced by the Erastianism and humanism of the period. A herculean task in itself, here
was a creative theology in the making.

As a bridge between the old and the new theologies, Wesley's
thought appears to be more creative than George Cell would credit
him, since Wesley had theological abutments both in the Reformation and the newer school of empiricism, with man at the center of all
critical thought. Respecting the latter, Wesley may even be said to
have anticipated the emphasis of Schleiermacher without letting the
subjective element become too authoritative, since it must rest on the
objective authority of the Word, as the Reformers had stressed. In
this respect, Wesley was very much ahead of his time.

A strong case can be made, we believe, for what we have referred
to as Wesley's bipolar position. It is to be contended in this light that
Wesley held to a powerful dialectics that put him in complete agree-
ment neither with Luther's dualism, on one hand, nor with Aquinas's
synthetic realism, on the other. Or, to pose the dialectical issue so
as to be more in keeping with expressed issues in theology today,
Wesley would stand neither with a realistic synthesis or absolute
idealism, on the one hand, nor with a completely Kierkegaardian dialectic, on the other, while appreciating the main points of both. For
him faith and reason were a working team; however, a faith based
on the revelation of the New Testament was not symphonic with a
natural philosophy or theology. Only a faith-conditioned reason
would be serviceable to God in the fullest Christian sense.

The bipolar perspective of Wesley can be seen perhaps more
clearly when one surveys his basic doctrinal emphases. In fact, it will
be reflected throughout the subsequent chapters, and the writer would
alert the reader to this Wesleyan dialectic. Neither stressing a rational synthesis of opposite principles, on the one hand, nor over-
accentuating them in an either/or type of dialectic, on the other, Wesley, we contend, asserts a paradoxical dialectic more in keeping with
a both/and tension. In such a dialectic, we have a bifocal view of
the basic issues at stake in theological doctrine, so as neither to abro-
gate the opposites belonging to the divine and human poles respectively, nor to fuse them rationally. That is to say, the opposites retain
their distinctiveness while being interrelated only under grace so as

to be mutually relevant. The divine remains divine, while the human remains human and finite, while redeemed *by*, and *made* serviceable, to the divine.

To epitomize Wesley's creative dialectics, we might describe it as a both/and tension in which both the absolute and relative, the divine and the human, the infinite and the finite, are retained, yet seen to be pertinent each to the other. Thus the transcendent and the immanent meet in both continuity and discontinuity. This provides for man as a creature of need as well as of possibility under God, even as it provides for both the saving God of grace and the relevant God of the faith experience.

More explicitly, the doctrinal aspects of Wesley's dialectics may be seen in the following issues: Wesley's more Arminian theology enables him to retain—

respect for man's moral freedom, yet the primacy of grace
justification by faith, yet holiness unto salvation
divine transcendence, yet divine immanence
man's depravity, yet a prevenient grace
righteousness by faith, yet righteousness by life
justified sinners, yet sinning Christians
voluntary sin, yet involuntary sin
a sovereign God, yet no election
biblical authority, yet subjective assurance
substitutionary atonement, yet continuous atonement
the new creature in Christ, yet taints of the old creature
sin as a propensity, yet sin as an act
sin as guilt, yet sin as a state
the witness of God's Spirit, yet the witness of our spirit
objective revelation, yet subjective witness
divine initiative, yet human choice
a God-given faith, yet the individual's faith
prevenient grace, yet grace by faith
the justified sinner, yet the cleansed believer.

Here it is noteworthy that the close-to-Pelagian view held by Wesley earlier in his career, prior to Aldersgate, is greatly qualified by the view of grace set forth in Paul's Epistle to the Romans. It is significant that at the Aldersgate meeting the leader read from Martin Luther's *Commentary* on this epistle. Thus as the message registered on Wesley's soul, we cannot overlook the dialectical issue that was almost bound to take shape in his mind, namely, the combination of divine grace and human freedom and experience. In this respect, George Cell is right in accentuating what Wesley had in common with the Reformers, yet his over-all argument is imbalanced, for Wesley never forsook but reorientated the strong points in his Anglican and pietistic backgrounds. In this respect, Wesley's thought drew closer to the theology of James Arminius, who had set a provocative precedent in maintaining a bipolar position respecting grace and freedom. This opened up a fresh and creative approach to Christian theology.

The main focal point of faith was shifted from man to God; nevertheless, in general, Wesley still held to his earlier views concerning man's moral capacity and its role in the divine-human encounter. However, it is the "prevenient grace" of God by which all men are made subjects of the saving grace of God that accounts for this active role, even as it opens up a potentially universal salvation without predetermining it. Prevenient grace enables the sinner to respond to the Word in penitence, and thus receive the faith of a new relationship. Righteousness is now seen to be as active as it is passive, that it is both possible and is acceptable to God. Dialectically, the shift from the primacy of the manward pole to the Godward demanded a wholesome adjustment in Wesley's theology. It opened up a creative bipolar position to which the God-manhood of Christ was both the inspiration and the theological corollary.

Contrary to some opinions, especially those of several critics of the last century who were prone to overstress the empirical and naturalistic aspects of religion at the expense of the transcendent element, much constructive theology and progressive thought came out of the Evangelical Awakening led by Wesley. While this qualifies notions held by some of the "progressive" liberal thinkers of the last century, it also challenges the more traditional types of orthodox system builders. As George Cell states: "There is an ancient and deep-seated prejudice that only an elaborate, scholastic theology can reveal the power of a great thinker on religious subjects."[5]

Adolf von Harnack may have been right to some degree when he asserted, at the turn of this century, that every great forward movement in Christianity has been characterized by a return to "the

---

[5] Cell, *op. cit.*, p. 16. Cf. pp. 8–14.

simple religion" of the historical Jesus. But Harnack appears to be as wrong as he was right. To be familiar with theological developments since Harnack's time is to understand the failure of the search for the objectively historical Jesus that would give a basis to the return to the simpler religion of an idealized teacher whose views are thought to be essentially moral. What has developed since, especially under the leadership of neo-Reformed thinkers such as Karl Barth and Emil Brunner under the influence of Sören Kierkegaard, has been a great resurgence of Protestant theology, both critically and constructively brought up to date. But this movement, which many, including the present writer, believe to be one of the most stimulating in theological history, is far from as simple as the theologies of the nineteenth century represented by Ritschl and Harnack. Harnack, again, may have been right in appealing to a simpler religion, but he seems to have overlooked the fact that the resurgence of religion under the Wesleys for instance, was far more than moral idealism.

Similarly, Wesley's theological adjustments may have catered somewhat to a simpler religion than some had held in his day, but a close examination of his position does not warrant the conclusion that his theology proper was "simple," let alone simple-minded. Too much prejudice has filled the air, and still lurks in some quarters, over the failure to grasp the power of Wesley's creativity as a theologian. And it may well be that Wesley's thinking had much more in common with the neo-Reformation movement in Protestant theology of this century than those still clinging to classical, pietistic and liberal Protestant traditions dare to believe.

Wesley tried to communicate with the mind of his day. Just as much in today's theology communicates with the contemporary mind through the existential perspective, so Wesley was constrained to communicate with the thinking of a strongly empirical perspective. Contemporary criticism did much to demand an empirical, experiential type of discourse, and Wesley accepted the challenge rather than run away from it. For him a vital religion of ample authority and meaning was to be found in the interaction between historical Christianity and men's personal lives. Theologically as well as evangelistically, Wesley proved himself a prophetic voice in the Age of the Enlightenment. He remained within the perspective of his age without succumbing to its humanistic and deistic weaknesses. This called for much reappraisal, theologically speaking, and to this John Wesley was by no means averse.

George Cell is correct in showing that Wesley has much in common with Luther and Calvin. Surely Wesley was a Protestant and not a Pelagian. This offsets much of the nineteenth-century trend to interpret the mature Wesley as the antithesis of Calvin, and a thinker but slightly aligned with Luther while rooted in the Catholic tradition of the Anglican Church. Yet, again, Cell seems to overdraw his conclusions, for there is little doubt that Wesley was steeped in the Anglican tradition, re-evaluated its doctrines, and even corrected the current trends within his Church under the influence of a distorted type of Arminianism. It were better to say that Wesley's theological adjustments and creativity amounted to an empirically adapted doctrine of the kind asserted by James Arminius, in Holland, back in the 1600's, which historically made a profound impression upon Anglican thought. Arminius's position was that of a more balanced Protestant, who saw a bipolar relationship between the primacy of divine grace and the involved freedom of man.[6] The Church of Wesley's day had succumbed largely to a moralistic and humanistic Pelagianism, but this emphasis must never be confused with genuine Arminianism. This is something that interpreters in both the more classical and modern schools of Protestant theology have been much too prone to miss or obscure.

In the first decade of his ministry after Aldersgate, Wesley was overtly opposed to the Calvinistic doctrine of predestination, but this gives no warrant for claiming that he severed his ties with the Reformation, either Continental or British. Thirty years later he could not hold so strongly to anti-Calvinism. Not that his thinking became typically Calvinistic, but his many contacts with Calvinists made him more appreciative of their theological intentions. Like James Arminius and John Fletcher, Wesley sought to embrace the fellowship of the Calvinists whether or not they opposed him theologically or castigated him, as some did. Wesley knew that he was in accord with them basically, due to a mutual regard for the primacy

---

[6] The writer intends to enlarge his interpretation in another work, *James Arminius and His Theology.*

of divine grace. To appreciate this, together with Wesley's concern for the moral freedom of man, is to understand that his position was a creative, bipolar one that can be described, though not necessarily defined, as a semi-Pelagianism. But in view of that same dialectics it can just as readily be said that Wesley was semi-Calvinist! Perhaps startling to some at first thought, this is no extremism, for Wesley always asserted man's basic need of grace. Even his Arminian references to "prevenient grace" all the more accentuates the matter, for in his post-Aldersgate theology Wesley refrained from describing sinful man as in any way being meritorious of divine blessing. A closer look at the theology of James Arminius gives some support to this principle also, because as much as Arminius resisted the starchy, stiff Calvinism of his day, he never claimed to withdraw from the main concerns of the Calvinists so much as he qualified their extremisms. Just as Arminius was of Protestant theological lineage, after all, so was Wesley, to a great degree, theologically speaking.

After Aldersgate, when Wesley found himself a believer, preacher and interpreter of the evangelical Gospel, he radically opposed the distorted type of Arminianism prevalent in the Church of England at that time, a kind not true to Arminius but more akin to Pelagius, with whom Augustine clashed back in the fourth century. Wesley held to a truer Arminianism, which maintained that Christian salvation is something of a God-given, God-inspired faith linked with the revelation of the Word and the immanent activity of the Holy Spirit. In this respect, Cell is quite right in saying, "Wesley's interest is plainly an anxious concern not to correct Calvinism but to rediscover and bring back Arminianism to evangelical principles."[7] Though this statement is quite sound, it is still subject to some misunderstanding. Cell would have been more accurate had he spoken of Wesley's theological concern bringing back a *distorted* Arminianism to evangelical principles. We make this qualification, because it must not be minimized, first, that Wesley was subordinately concerned about correcting Calvinism at the point of its doctrine of predestination, and, second, that the so-called Arminianism to which Cell refers in this context was not the true Arminianism of its author, but of a contemporary Anglicanism, which not only had become largely moral-

---

[7] Cell, *op. cit.*, pp. 5–8.

istic but coldly deistic and indifferent to the masses. In fact, Wesley was far more alarmed about the latter than about the Calvinism which he found it necessary to attack doctrinally on occasion. As Cannon recognizes,[8] Wesley saw himself but "a hair's breadth from Calvinism," since both schools of thought looked to the primacy of grace, while Wesley stood toward it in a more synergistic, functional sense because of his doctrine of prevenient grace.

Cell is correct in asserting that Wesley's evangelical principles consisted in (1) ascribing all good to the free grace of God, (2) denying all natural free will and all power antecedent to grace, and (3) excluding all merit from man, even for what he has or does under divine grace.[9] In view of the above, including our qualifications of Cell's interpretation of Wesley, we concur with him in the following statement, which is directed not only against the *distorted* Anglican Arminianism of Wesley's day, but that of more recent generations as well:

> Wesley in the epoch of his maturity never was an Arminian as that term is now more commonly taken and accepted. Wesley would reject as decisively the current Arminianism of Methodist theology today [1930's] as he rejected the current Arminianism of Anglican theology of his own time and for the same reasons. As he saw it, Anglican theology, decidedly Arminian had "run from Calvinism as far as ever it could, whereas the truth of the Gospel lies within a hair's breadth of Calvinism" . . . Anglican teaching . . . no longer had a gospel to preach, certainly not one which is the power of God unto *salvation* to every believer. Wesley, therefore, after exploring this [distorted] Arminian theology for over ten years, concluded that it was a byway of spiritual despair and fatality, not a highway of saving faith and Christian perfection and went back in his search for power to the Luther-Calvin idea of God-given faith.[10]

This blends with our contention in the previous chapter that Aldersgate was for Wesley a spiritual renewal, because it was a doctrinal awakening that, in turn, made for a complete theological reorientation. It centered in a Protestant clarification of a basic Pauline emphasis. Cell is right in what he says here, including his inference that

---

[8] Cannon, *op. cit.*, Chapter 4.

[9] *Ibid.*

[10] *Ibid.*, p. 25.

the Methodist theology of this century, especially a few decades back, shifted too far to the left in its anthropological implications, so as to become not the Arminian theology that Wesley would defend, but that he would actually resist. Much in nineteenth-century Methodist theology represented a gradual shift from free grace to free will, as Robert Chiles has brought out. This shift is one represented most noticeably in the movements of thought from the Methodist theologian Watson to John Miley to Albert Knudson.[11] Parallel to this trend, and giving it support, was a growing philosophy and theology of immanence like that topped off by Hegelian theologies and the Bostonian personalism of the earlier decades of this century.

Wesley held to an immanental view of God but without neglecting or obscuring the meaning of divine transcendence. God was for him in his creation like a mind in a body, but He is also objectively real and not limited to His creation. Today, neo-Reformation theology has appeared to offset the extreme, man-centered versions of immanence which dominated last-century thought. The "infinite qualitative difference" between God and man has been asserted by Karl Barth under the influence of Kierkegaard. Though Wesley's dialectical position would not support Barth's either/or type of dialectics, he would greatly appreciate Barth's reappraisal of the Reformed view of the primacy of grace. Yet the strong dichotomy in Barth's views between divine transcendence and man's sinful finitude would cause Wesley to wonder whether the role of man in salvation had been utterly negated. The bipolar issue is reasonably expressed by Gerald Ensley, when he states: "There may be nothing which John Calvin taught about man's present status which is too pessimistic. But there is likewise nothing which John Wesley taught about God's power to redeem which is too optimistic."[12]

To reiterate our thesis, Wesley was truly a creative theologian in his day, to have come forth with such a communicative bipolar scheme. His dialectics preserved the man in need who was sinful in

---

11 Cf., Robert Chiles, "Methodist Apostasy: From Free Grace to Free Will," in *Religion in Life*, Summer, 1958.

12 F. Gerald Ensley, *John Wesley, Evangelist*, p. 35. Wesley's dialectics as related to this very matter open up wholesome possibilities for the theological ecumenicity of the Church. For the practical implications of this, see Colin Williams, *Wesley's Theology Today*.

condition and station, while addressible and salvageable not on his own terms but on those of God. Divine grace was seen to be central without usurping the role of man, especially his freedom to respond, lest salvation be to no glory of the Lord, on the one hand, and to no pseudo-glory of man, on the other. At the same time the God–man relationship was preserved in such a way as to be consistently dependent upon God, while righteousness was as activated as it was imputed, the latter being basic to the justified believer's status and the former basic to the redeemed man's new affections and responsibilities. It is this that prevented Wesley from being too confident in the natural man, while at the same time not being too restrictive of redeemed man. For him salvation was not only *from* sin but *to* the higher life, both aspects being dependent upon the Word and the Spirit.

CHAPTER VI

THE DOCTRINAL CONTENT OF WESLEY'S THEOLOGY

(I)

THOUGH THE Wesleyan Awakening was a profoundly personal appeal to men and a movement of marked social consequence, it must never be overlooked that it was positively theological in its undergirdings. Wesley believed in a sovereign God who deals with men and creation on his own terms. Such a God is the very soul of the universe, Wesley believed, while more than the cosmic process itself. Both immanent and transcendent, God to Wesley was an objective, infinite being by no means identifiable with a humanistic projection of men's highest ideals. Nor was God so transcendent of his creation as to be aloof from it, as in the prevalent deism of Wesley's day. Thus neither sheer naturalism nor an objectified idealism, let alone a self-sufficient humanism, can be ascribed to any aspect of Wesley's evangelical theology with its emphasis upon salvation by faith as meaningful here and now.

GOD AND MAN

For John Wesley the universe was not to be interpreted as limited to any kind of mechanistic theory. God as immanental to the universe was to be understood as the soul of the universe, and this, in turn, implied that nature is a system of forces administered intelligently and purposefully to moral ends.[1] The corollary of this is man as the highest of earthly creatures. God as transcendent to the universe was understood as a divine power and person who can sus-

---

[1] George C. Cell, *The Rediscovery of John Wesley*, p. 303.

pend natural law, if necessary, for all such law is under his jurisdiction. Miracles are not inconceivable, Wesley believed, although they ceased in the third century due to man's waning love for God. Ahead of his time, Wesley saw the problem of mechanistic determinism looming large under the guise of an encroaching eighteenth-century naturalism, which was being released by the current scientific trends of thought. He shrewdly saw the possibility of a dangerous relationship between a mechanistic philosophy of the cosmos and a necessitarian psychology unwittingly supported in some respects by the predestinarian doctrine of the Calvinists.[2] The nineteenth century bore out the mechanistic trend as the theory of scientific determinism gained momentum, and the moral freedom and mental nature of man were increasingly put in question. This is seen clearly in such emphases as Newtonian physics, the mechanistic determinism of Joseph Priestley, the evolutionary theories stemming from Charles Darwin, and later an increasingly behavioristic psychology and positivistic sociology.

Wesley held that divine revelation and redemption are necessary to man's salvation. They proceed from the perfect goodness, justice and power of God, properties that belong solely to the sovereignty of the Lord. The great evangelist of the eighteenth century, therefore, told the church of his day that a rationalistic theory of a remote, deistic God is no better than none. Rather, God is the universal, Christlike Father who can be confronted by faith as one who welcomes man's spiritual communion. In this context, Wesley was a firm believer in the orthodox doctrine of the Trinity, yet he made no serious contentions about its doctrinal intricacies.[3] His theologizing was related more to the soteriological doctrines. Both the depravity of man and the divine causality of redemption were strongly affirmed by Wesley so that the absolute necessity of God's grace and Spirit were germane to his soteriology. This fact should not be obscured or overlooked, as it sometimes is, by overplaying the strong ethical implications of Wesley's doctrine of salvation. Wesley would not have it so.

Wesley saw that for Christians the final authority of their faith

---

2 Umphrey Lee, *John Wesley and Modern Religion*, pp. 113–17, 127.

3 *Ibid.* Cf. Cell, *op. cit.*, pp. 253–301, 25–34.

and hope is found in the Bible and confirmed by Christian experience. In this respect, Wesley was definitely a "Bible Christian" to the core, but this did not make him averse to the critical inquiry and exegesis of the Scriptures. As a theologian and preacher Wesley also had a high regard for the works of the ante-Nicene fathers of the early Church. Well stated are the words of Umphrey Lee:

> It has been too easily assumed that Wesley simply reinstated ortho-dox theology and the letter of the Bible as Christian infallibilities, or that he set up Christian experience as a final authority. The truth is that he felt the richness of Christian truth to be too great to allow so simple a solution.[4]

Neither the letter of the Bible, the historic creeds nor religious experience, each in itself, could supply the entire truth for Wesley. Rather, the message of the Word, the historic and homiletical clarification of its doctrinal implications and the high moments of personal faith as existentially vital to life were all correlative. Either without the other would be immature or incomplete, theologically. Thus we begin to see the well-rounded "wholeness" of Wesley's theological perspective.

As for the nature of man, Wesley saw him to be "one species in a chain of being which stretches from the plants to man." The division between man and animals was seen to be far more than a mental category. Man is created *imago dei,* in the image of God. Man is spirit in a material body, a creature having understanding, will, affections and moral freedom. As such, man is addressible by God, and God is knowable by man, though solely on God's own man-related terms of grace. In contrast, animals cannot know God or love him. Man is distinctive as a creature under God.

ORIGINAL SIN

But original sin enters the picture as a serious problem in the God–man relationship, as Wesley sees it. In the Adamic Fall man lost "the moral image of God" and to some measure "the natural image." The former refers to the broken relationship that only God can re-

---

[4] *Ibid.,* pp. 143, 130 ff.

store; the latter, the defectiveness or infirmity, though not the loss, of man's capacities as a man.[5] In this respect we might say, by way of interpolation, that man is depraved totally but not totally depraved; that is, he is spiritually limited and distorted, even perverse in his fleshly state, but as a man before God he is still a man, one whom God addresses as such. He is out of harmonious relationship with God as a sinner, but he is still addressible and salvageable as a spiritual being. Though man's back be turned, he can hear God's call. In this respect, the disunion implied by the Fall becomes man's inability to reflect God's likeness or image in and of himself, but when God addresses man in his Word, man can respond positively through faith's dependence upon that grace-initiated address.

Having abused his liberty, Adam (man) chose evil, and thus lost the image of God, morally. This defect, with its limitations, implies the disposition of human nature now to succumb to evil (Cf. Romans 7), as the historic orthodox view had long maintained. Wesley could see that original sin is the doctrinal expression of the problem of man in his sinful state, or of the so-called natural man. This state was not due merely to man's earthly conditioning through habit, custom, poor training or bad environment; it was due, rather, to man's defective human nature inherited from Adam. In this respect, Wesley's view was largely in keeping with the orthodox, medieval Traducian theory, which even held the human blood stream to be a sewerline of corruption. Wesley held that man was depraved to the extent that, despite his talents, capacities and the spiritual endowments accompanying a "prevenient grace," with such concomitants as a normal conscience, he is sinfully biased. Thus man does what he does because he is what he is. Yet man does not understand this of himself. He neither understands it nor admits it, apart from divine revelation.

Man's ego, with its self-concern, is bent in pride or self love, Wesley saw. Adam is the representative man, and more. He rebelled against God, sacrificing his innocence out of self-gratification. At the Fall, this introduced not only sinful guilt but pain, death, and disjunction from God. By it all mankind is fallen through the "in-

---

[5] John Wesley, "Original Sin," and "Justification by Faith," in Wesley's *Works*, Vol. I. Cf. *Sermons on Several Occasions*, Vol. I (1794).

herited corruption." Though not a new problem theologically, Wesley does not seem to account for how an originally good nature could go wrong; likewise the transmission of a state of sin through natural propagation, when the original Adamic sin was moral in form. These become big problems, especially for thinkers who, like Wesley, settle for neither predestination nor a Supralapsarian or pre-Fall view of the redemptive plan, on the one hand, while retaining the vital role of man in the divine–human relation, on the other. Even so, the problem addressed by the theory of original sin is not to be ignored by men today any more than it was by Wesley in his day, for it bespeaks the universality of sin, its profound influence on all of life, and how it is even a problem for the regenerate man, who therefore must be perennially dependent upon God's grace. Today, the problem still prevails but demands a different interpretation, the shrewdest being that of an existential perspective such as is seen in the works of theologians like Karl Barth, Emil Brunner and Reinhold Niebuhr.

As orthodox as Wesley was respecting original sin, he was almost ahead of his time in recognizing the empirical and social aspects of evil. Human problems multiply in a social context, he saw. Yet social evils are the result of human nature, Wesley believed. Man's free will is weak or infirm when his affections are not guided by divine understanding. Here is where Christian ethics becomes a matter both of personal and social significance for Wesley. Few theologians prior to Wesley reckoned with this aspect of sin.

VOLITIONAL SIN

Volitional or willful sin is distinguishable from original sin, Wesley asserted. In this he is quite Johannine, even as he reflects a theology akin to that of James Arminius, with some precedents in Thomas Aquinas. Volitional sin is the more responsible aspect of man's rebelliousness.[6] Though Adam's posterity has a sinful bias or disposition, a perversion of the originally innocent nature of man, this bias does not imply that man's faculties of freedom and con-

---

[6] Cf. Lee, *op. cit.*, pp. 118–22, 124–28.

science as well as reason are negated. The sinful bias constrains human freedom but does not eliminate it, lest there be no moral will at all. Free will is intact, but seriously limited by the fleshly state. Sometimes, then, the will capitulates to the sinful disposition or makes evil choices. This applies not only to the sinner but to the Christian as well. Choices contrary to divine will or law constitute volitional sin, corresponding to what John speaks of as the breaking of a known law of God (I John 3:4, 24). Volitional sin amounts to a willful breaking of the revealed will of God as found in the Old Testament, especially the Decalogue, and the New Testament ethics, especially the teachings of Jesus.

The Christian sometimes submits to volitional sin through failure to rely upon God's regenerating grace. Self-sufficiency may lead not only to forms of error and pride but outright sin. The element of deliberation is paramount, in the sense that a choice was involved in the act, word or thought. Error or ignorance are excepted in this case, since volitional sin is a more specific and deliberate type of sin that many things intrinsic to the fleshly state or to social conditioning might imply. The Christian must repent of volitional sin and seek grace afresh; in fact, he can hardly repent of anything of which he is unaware.

One thing that this distinction does for the Christian is to keep him aware of the closeness of sin and guilt in a way not conducive to a mere acknowledgment of sin as a fleshly state in which everyone is involved. The latter is important, but unless qualified this way may lead to the attitude, "How can I help it?" or to the semi-indifference of "everyone does it." The greater particularity of volitional sin drives the believer to his knees with a more pronounced sense of divine dependence. Wesley suggested that slovenliness in devotional life may lead to a "fall from grace" even after one tastes of the regenerating and sanctifying Spirit. This is because such negligence bespeaks self-sufficiency, rather than a conscious reliance upon God and his grace. The apostle at least adumbrated the idea when he said to the Galatian Church: "Ye have fallen from grace." Concrete human experience corroborates it sometimes, as in the case of the seaman who said to two church workers: "Let no one overlook the possibility. I was once happy in the grace of God. Today, when the Word is preached or prayed, I am as hard as a stone."

At this point Wesley differed considerably from the Calvinists of his day, inasmuch as he gave a larger place to man's role in communion with God. The doctrine of "eternal security" or "perseverance" held by Calvinists blended with their doctrine of predestination, stressing that God does not withdraw his grace, therefore the man of faith cannot fall from grace. Wesley could appreciate the God-centered aspect of such a soteriology, but he contended that, though God does not withdraw his grace, and even extends some measure of it to all men, persons of faith can be overwhelmed by temptations and volitionally succumb to the extent of withdrawing from grace or turning their backs on God through a neglect or disregard of his grace, which alone can defeat the flesh. Thus God may ever extend his grace, but the tempted or negligent may still spurn it. God never constrains men but persuades and inspires them, without violating their manhood with its moral and spiritual constitution. To violate man's constitution *qua* man would be to no glory of God, who created man as one with whom he could have fellowship.

Wesley contended that for a person to neglect the means of grace is to cater to, or rely upon, a human will that is still apt to be weak in the face of temptation. Hence spiritual discipline is important to the Christian. Not to repent of sin is in itself a stifling of the Holy Spirit's essential work, since it is a lack of dependence upon the Spirit. Original sin, then, is the condition, the setting, or the occasion for volitional sin. Both are brought under control only through the sanctifying work of the Spirit (Romans 8). The man of faith perseveres in grace only as he yields to it and relies on it, or responds responsibly to its promptings. Thus grace is ever essential without being coercive.

PREVENIENT GRACE

As serious as is original sin or corruption, Wesley contends that no man in a state of nature is wholly void of God's grace. He would hardly be a man in such a case. No man, not even the fallen, natural

man, is entirely destitute of "natural conscience," for example. This
is due to what Wesley calls "prevenient grace," or the grace that
precedes or *goes before*, sometimes known as "preventing grace."
This implies, in turn, that a man sins not because he lacks grace but
because he does not depend upon the grace that is extended to him.
Man can do no good thing apart from grace. Prevenient grace implies that even the unjustified sinner is dependent upon God for any
practical good or virtue, even that of repentance and faith itself.

As George Cell states:

> Wesley . . . well knew the other half of the better story of Man's
> personal life. It is covered in his doctrine of "prevenient grace," of
> which he had a firm grasp in all the stages of his ministry. It is
> given in his profound insight into the divine, the diviner and the
> divinest immanence. Briefly he taught that no human being ever es-
> capes the beneficent presence of the living God. Not only are all the
> human springs of moral goodness in God, but human life at its
> worst is never without a positive principle of goodness in it. And
> then at its best, religion is "the life of God in the soul of man." So
> then his black picture of humanity need not be misleading, unless,
> as usually happens, it is dissevered from his all-embracing doctrine
> of the divine immanence, and divorced from its distinctly religious
> motivation and meaning. Then of course it becomes at once absurd
> and repulsive. But this understanding of Wesley is without excuse.
> Viewing as he did all nature as a system of forces utterly plastic
> and freely administered to moral ends, he lived and moved and had
> his being in the presence of God.[7]

Thus Wesley both retains and qualifies the moral dilemma that
human depravity implies. The "natural man" who is utterly corrupt
constitutionally is for Wesley a kind of "logical fiction," since even
he has the "plus" of grace, that is, prevenient grace, without which he
could not even understand the gospel or appropriate its justifying
and regenerating grace. The natural man does not have an innate
knowledge of God, especially as conducive to a divine-human fellowship, but he does have some possibility for good in God.[8] Prevenient
grace is what provides for this and is important to Wesley, inasmuch
as it retains both the primacy of the divine initiative and man's
responsive dependence upon its redemptiveness. It also makes the

---

[7]Cell, *op. cit.*, p. 303.

[8] Lee, *op. cit.*, pp. 124–28.

good that man seeks in God quite distinctive from what might be called the natural good linked with creation more than with redemption. Thus man, though sinful, has the prevenient grace, that, if relied upon, will enable him to seek, understand, repent, have faith and respond to the regenerating grace essential to the Christian life. In our day, Francis Thompson has articulated it poetically in his "Hound of Heaven."

But a problem looms large between the lines: .Cannot the Calvinist even press this distinction to the point of saying that since the sinner is dependent upon the grace of God, regardless of how you classify or describe it functionally, you cannot avoid some form of election or predestination? Wesley's reply would be respectful but to the contrary, inasmuch as he is still strongly asserting the role of man. God takes the initiative, true, but only as He chooses to self-limit himself to deal with man as a moral-spiritual being such as He has created him to be. On this basis man is responsive, since God's love is initial. On this basis, too, neither man's calling nor his perseverance is automatic, so to speak. For God to operate in a moral context of this kind is no limitation to His sovereignty, for He has morally self-willed such a relation, even self-limited Himself to do it. Thus God capacitates man and even aids man, but does not coerce him. It is prevenient grace that helps capacitate or dispose the sinner to repent.

To understand this much is enough in itself to understand how Wesley's theological dialectics was truly creative in his day. Though having precedent in the theology of James Arminius and the pattern, though not the ontology, of Thomas Aquinas, Wesley employs a less stringent logic than Luther and Calvin, with respect to the initiating function of divine grace. Since this is more realistic and empirical in context, the doctrinal content is bound to call for a more subtle dialectics. This is because Wesley prefers to do justice to the bipolar factors of both God and man, as seen in Chapter V, since he sees them not only in relation but in a relationship.

Wesley's theological structure is not one of Scholastic ontology or rational theory so much as an empirical and pre-existential setting. In this light Wesley is to be accused of neither a rational synthesis nor an easy-going, optimistic synergism. Rather, here is a both/and tension of a paradoxical nature that protects both the distinctiveness of a necessary grace, on the one hand, and a morally capacitated and conditioned man, on the other, while also protecting the meaning of their relationship both as continuity and discontinuity. To understand this is to be careful not to abuse Wesley's position either from a more conservative right or a more liberal left.

FREE GRACE

In his great sermon on "Free Grace," based on Romans 8:32, John Wesley emphasizes that God's grace is free and for all. In discussing this, the question of predestination eventually comes up, concerning which Wesley states:

> Call it therefore by whatever name you please, election, preterition, predestination, or reprobation, it comes in the end to the same thing. The sense of all is plainly this: by virtue of an eternal, unchangeable, irresistible decree of God, one part of mankind are infallibly saved; and the rest infallibly damned; it being impossible that any of the former should be damned, or that any of the latter should be saved. But if this be so, then is all preaching vain.[9]

Predestination, Wesley believed, is also a doctrine that tends to destroy holiness, the true happiness of Christianity, the complete assurance, the zeal of good works, the missionary spirit, in fact, the whole Christian revelation by making it contradict itself. Wesley's sermon "On Predestination" was centered on Romans 8:29, 30. In it he states the following:

> . . . the apostle is not here (as many as have supposed) describing a chain of causes and effects; but simply showing *the method in which God works*, the order in which the several branches of salvation constantly follow each other . . . The first point is the foreknowledge of God. God foreknew . . . who would believe, from the beginning of the world to the consummation of all things . . . when we speak of God's foreknowledge we do not speak according to the nature of things, but after the manner of men. For if we speak properly, there is no such thing as either foreknowledge or after knowledge in God . . . he does not know one thing before another, or one

---

[9] Wesley, *Works*, Vol. I, p. 483.

thing after another; but sees all things in one point of view, from everlasting to everlasting . . .[10]

It is noteworthy that at this point Wesley has much in common with the existential perspective of the Eternal Now seen in the existential type of theology of our day. He goes on to say of the divine knowledge of things and events:

> But observe: we must not think they are because he knows them. No, he knows them, because they are . . . In like manner, God knows that man sins, for he knows all things; yet we do not sin because he knows it, but he knows it because we sin . . . his knowledge . . . does not in any way cause it . . . Men are as free in believing, or not believing, as if he did not know it at all . . . whom he did foreknow, them he did predestinate to be conformed to the image of his Son . . . God decrees from everlasting to everlasting, that all who believe in the Son of his love, shall be conformed to his image; shall be saved from all inward and outward sin, into all inward and outward holiness . . .[11]

It should be apparent that Wesley's doctrine of "free grace" articulates both man's dependence on the initiative of God's reconciling grace as a gift, while strongly asserting the functional setting as moral in nature—not as human merit but as appropriation of what is freely given to "whosoever believeth" (John 3:16).

ATONEMENT

Among John Wesley's many writings there is no discourse devoted to the subject of the atonement, though his sermons are replete with references to it. The essence of the New Testament message was to him faith unto salvation through God's redeeming grace. Jesus came to save sinners, and the center of faith is the sacrifice of Christ, reflective of the free grace of God to all men. Akin to the Reformers, Wesley emphasized an objective atonement through the cross. This became especially meaningful to him after his 1738 Aldersgate experience. In the face of this doctrine, the Fall of man is understood

[10] *Ibid.*, Vol. II, p. 39.

[11] *Ibid.* Concerning the preceding comment of comparison, see the author's work *Time and Its End* (Vantage Press, N. Y., 1962).

in a new light, for Wesley says, almost daringly, that humanity is
not the "loser" but the "gainer" by the Fall.[12] It is as if Wesley were
giving specification to the idea that man does not know or appreciate
the good until he has tasted of evil.

George Croft Cell significantly states:

> We must then have ever in mind Wesley's appraisal of the Christian
> revelation and atonement, while we consider his very dark view of
> man as the subject of redemption. All criticism, even the most friend-
> ly, agrees that the Wesleyan picture of human nature in terms of
> original sin and total depravity is extremely dark. The most sympa-
> thetic and appreciative interpreter will have to understand and ap-
> praise it in the light of its purely religious purpose. Its one sole
> purpose is to make away with a godless humanistic religion and to
> destroy root and branch the proud pretension of human reason to be
> the self-sufficient architect of all righteousness, all moral goodness
> in man. Its master aim is to magnify the grace of God and to bring
> every man, a sinner in need of a savior, in utter humility to the foot
> of the cross of Christ. Viewed objectively without reference to its
> origin in and dependence upon the Christian consciousness, the Wes-
> leyan representation of human nature would certainly be one-sided.[13]

The conventional "substitutionary theory" of the atonement was
maintained by Wesley, but the love of God was to him the primary
factor in the doctrine.[14] The doctrine of "divine immanence," Wesley
realized, did not fully harmonize with "total depravity" in man, as
hinted above; hence his more temperate views of original sin as
loss of the moral image together with the function of prevenient
grace. As previously set forth, he maintained an orginal sin that
corrupts man as it breaks the God–man relationship but without
destroying man's capacities or nature as man. No man is void entirely
of God's grace, yet there is nothing in the entire universe that is good
outside of God's grace. Thus Wesley divided saving faith into two
parts: the finished and the unfinished work of Christ. The finished
work, as vindicated in the resurrection, is all that God in Christ has
done for man's salvation. The unfinished work is all that God continues to do in the collective experience of the Christian Church and

---

[12] Lee, *op. cit.*, pp. 253–301.

[13] Cell, *op. cit.*, p. 303.

[14] Lee, *op. cit.*, p. 123.

its members, who look constantly to the finished work of the atonement.

Wesley does not limit the atonement, however, to the finished
work of Christ. It is complete, yet continues in its efficacy. Here
it is well to note how Wesley anticipates much in contemporary
theology, chiefly the emphasis upon the existential *presence* of the
divine Act. Though the past act of revelation is an important media-
tion, the crucial existential present of the God–man relationship is
paramount. Here "Wesley saw an objective element no less in God's
hand in the actual experience of saving faith than in the person and
work of Christ." Always he saw a theocentric view of Christian
experience and the Christian movement in history. Furthermore, as
George Cell has brought out, "He believed the goodness of God to
be no less clearly manifest in what is withheld from us than in
what is revealed to us."

Wesley's close-to-Calvinistic doctrine of grace as total dependence
upon God, and his Arminian (not Pelagian!) doctrine of human
freedom, which makes man a subject of action and moral obligation, do not really clash. Total dependence does not mean "an exclusive divine causality which swallows up all human responsibility."
Rather, the religious experience and source of inspiration are interrelated. "Dependence and freedom may be a rational logical contradiction, but not an experiential contradiction." For all we know,
dependence upon God might be "the birthplace, not the graveyard,
of personal freedom.[15] This is akin to Augustine's view of "liberty."
The "major liberty" in Christ is reached by grace, while not out of
relation to the "minor liberty" of man as a moral being.

Though Wesley held to a theocentric salvation, it included a
moral freedom, thus providing a "radical ethic of divine grace."
In this respect, Wesley had a more favorable view of Pelagius than
some medieval and Protestant thinkers have seen possible. Not a
Pelagian out and out, Wesley nevertheless gave credit to Pelagius
where he felt it was deserved. Of this Cell states: ". . . he gave
Pelagius right and censured Augustine harshly for his failure to
discern the relative truth and radical importance of the Pelagian

---

[15] Cell, *op. cit.*, pp. 304–9.

doctrine of holiness—the moral problem." Wesley saw too many people turning grace into what Saint Paul attacked as "license." He saw
many who "used the doctrine of grace as a dispensation from righteousness, a compensation for the lack of it and a city of refuge from
the guilt and penalty of evil-doing."[16]

Though this statement calls for careful consideration, it contains
a realistic truth. Wesley believed that the doctrine of Christ's righteousness as a *substitute* for man's holiness, instead of as an introduction to it, has done considerable harm. Wesley saw a spiritual "plus"
in salvation. Justification by faith is central to a relation with God,
true enough, but holiness as the spiritual and active Christian ethic
completes salvation, making it mature (Cf. Romans 12:1, 2). Salvation, then, *is* the Christian life. Faith without applied righteousness
is sterile. The Gospel does not only save men in sin, but from sin and
sinning. In Cell's words, "He [Wesley] construed the desire of forgiveness without the aspiration after ethical goodness or holiness as
the maximum of spiritual perversity. . . . The atonement, whatever
else it can mean, must mean the actual work of saving sinful men
into righteousness."[17] Redemption by way of the Cross is a "turning
about" from the old life to "the new creature in Christ."

THE SACRAMENTS

For the most part, Wesley never wavered in his allegiance to the
major doctrines of the Church of England. He held to the Bible, the
prayerbook, the three creeds and the Articles, though the latter he reduced from thirty-nine to twenty-seven. As for baptismal regeneration, he did not seem to deny it. However, when he associated regeneration with baptism he seemed to use the term figuratively, which
became a "philological rather than theological blunder," as Arthur
W. Little puts it. Wesley believed in Confirmation but rewrote the
Catechism. He regarded the Holy Eucharist as "a perpetual memory
of the one great Sacrifice on Calvary; that only a priest, episcopally

---

[16] *Ibid.*, pp. 304–43.
[17] *Ibid.*
[18] Arthur W. Little, *The Times and Teachings of John Wesley*, pp. 32–41.

ordained, can consecrate the Blessed Sacrament."[18] The Holy Communion was important to receive frequently, he maintained, as did the early Christians.[19]

Wesley says we are made children of God in baptism through grace and adoption. He says: "Herein a principle of grace is infused, which will not be wholly taken away, unless we quench the Holy Spirit of God by long-continued wickedness." Wesley did not forget this in his preaching to the baptized about new birth. He says that the baptized are born again, but we cannot comprehend how, whether in the young or in older persons. But only a *present* faith makes baptism effectual. It is not sufficient simply to say, "I was once baptized. Therefore I am now a child of God." Wesley bluntly states: "How many are the baptized gluttons and drunkards, the baptized liars and common swearers, the baptized railers and evil speakers, the baptized whore-mongers, thieves, extortioners? What think you? Are these now the children of God?" Stressing the need of personal regeneration, Wesley adds, "And if ye have been baptized, your hope is this, that those who were federally made the children of God by baptism, but are now the children of the devil, may yet receive power to become the sons of God."[20] Here we see reflected a practical application of the distinction between a prevenient and a regenerating grace. Only the latter is fully efficacious, as it were.

Wesley once stated in the most forthright terms: "The beginning of that vast, inward change is usually termed the New Birth. Baptism is the outward sign of this inward grace, which is supposed by our Church to be given with and through that sign to all infants, and to those of riper years, if they repent and believe the Gospel. But how entirely idle are the common disputes on this head! I tell a sinner, 'You must be born again!' 'No,' you say, 'he was born again in baptism; therefore, he cannot be born again.' Alas, what trifling is this! What if he was then a child of God? He is now manifestly a child of the devil; for the works of his father he doeth. Therefore do not play upon words. He must go through an entire change of heart. In one not yet baptized, you yourself would call that change the New Birth. In him, call it what you will, but remember

---

[19] J. H. Overton, *John Wesley*, pp. 69, 80.

[20] John Wesley, "The Marks of the New Birth," in *Sermons on Several Occasions*, Vol. I (1794), pp. 289 f.

meantime that if either he or you die without it, your baptism will
be so far from profiting you that it will increase your damnation."[21]

Here again we see how Wesley stresses the existential pertinence of
sound doctrine and discounts any theological hair-splitting not congenial to redemption as a truth of vital efficacy in this life.

JUSTIFICATION

In his sermon "Grace by Faith," based on Ephesians 2:18, John
Wesley states that all blessings received by man are solely of God's
favor and undeserved.[22] Man has no claim to God's mercy, and
righteousness is a gift. Man cannot atone for his sins, since his works
are vitiated just as he is. "Grace is the source, faith the condition,
of salvation," says Wesley. An outline of the sermon is worthy of
one's perusal.

I. *What faith is it through which we are saved?*
   1. It is not the faith of a heathen.
   2. It is not the faith of a devil.
   3. It is not even the faith like that of the apostles when Christ
      was yet upon earth.
   4. "It is a faith in Christ; Christ, and God through Christ, are
      the proper objects of it . . . For thus saith the Scripture.
      "With the heart man believeth unto righteousness." And "If
      thou shalt confess with thy mouth the Lord Jesus, and shalt
      believe with thy heart, that God hath raised him from the
      dead, thou shalt be saved."
   5. "And herein does it differ from that faith which the apostles
      themselves had while the Lord was on earth, that it ac-
      knowledge the necessity and merit of his death, and the
      power of his resurrection. It acknowledges his death as the
      only sufficient means of redeeming man from death eternal,
      and his resurrection as the restoration of us all to life and
      immortality; inasmuch as he 'was delivered for our sins, and
      rose again for our justification.' "
   6. "Christian faith is then, not only an assent to the whole Gos-
      pel of Christ, but also a full reliance on the blood of Christ;

---

[21] Cited by Overton, *op. cit.*, p. 78; cf. pp. 76 ff.; cf. Wesley's sermon "The
Marks of the New Birth."
[22] Wesley, *Works*, Vol. I, pp. 13–16.

a trust in the merits of his life, death, and resurrection; a recumbency upon him as our atonement and our life, as given for us, and living in us. It is a sure confidence which a man hath in God, that through the merits of Christ, his sins are forgiven, and he is reconciled to the favor of God; and in consequence hereof, a closing with him, and cleaving to him, as our 'wisdom, righteousness, sanctification, and redemption,' or in one word our salvation."

II. *What salvation is it, which comes through this faith?*
1. It is a present salvation.
2. Christ will save from all "original and actual, past and present sin." We are saved from both its guilt and power.
3. Christ has removed the curse of the law in "becoming a curse for us."
4. Men are thus saved from guilt, from fear of punishment and the wrath of God. "Received the spirit of adoption . . . Spirit bearing witness with our spirit . . . They are also saved from the fear, though not the possibility, of falling away from the grace of God."
5. Here Wesley quotes I John 3:5 f.
6. One born of God by this faith does not sin (1) by any habitual sin, (2) by willful sin, (3) by any sinful desire, (4) "by infirmities, whether in act, word or thought; for his *infirmities have no concurrence of his will, and without this they are not properly sins.*" [Note the plural term.]
7. This is expressed in the term "justification" so that "he who is thus justified, or saved by faith, is indeed born again."

III. *Answering objections to this.* This faith is not separate from holiness and good works, but "necessarily productive of all good works and all holiness."

In his sermon on "Justification by Faith," based on Romans 4:5, we note Wesley's more direct expression of this great doctrine.[23] An outline of the sermon is as follows:

I. *The ground of the doctrine of justification.*
1. Man was first created in the image of God, pure.
2. "It seemed good to the sovereign wisdom of God to superadd one positive law, "Thou shalt not eat of the fruit of the tree . . ."

---

[23] *Ibid.*, pp. 44–51.

3. In man's state of happiness man was to remain, if he continued to obey God, but if he did not, "In that day," said
   God, "ye shall surely die."
4. Man disobeyed God and was thus condemned by righteous
   judgment of God.
5. Thus "by one man sin entered into the world, and death by
   sin." All were made dead in sin by it. By Adam's sin all fell
   short of God's favor.
6. Another common head of mankind was made: The Son of
   God, who tasted of death for all.
7. Now God "reconciled the world unto himself, not imputing
   to them their former trespasses."

II. *What is justification?*
1. ". . . it is not the being made actually just and righteous.
   This is sanctification . . . The one implies what God 'does for
   us' through his Son; the other, what he 'works in us' by his
   Spirit."
2. Justification is "clearing us from the accusation brought
   against us by the law," so God does not inflict the punishment men deserve.
3. Justification is not thinking we are innocent.
4. Justification is pardon or forgiveness of sins of the past.

III. *Who are justified?*
1. "He justifieth the ungodly," sinners.
2. One need not be sanctified before he can be justified.
3. Justified are the lost of the "carnal mind" who believe.
4. Those "the burden of whose sins are intolerable."
5. Good deeds before justification are not acceptably good works
   in the sight of God, good works follow justification.

IV. *What terms justify?*
1. One alone, belief in him who justifieth the ungodly raising
   them from death to life.
2. "Faith in general is a divine *elegchos*, evidence or conviction
   of things not seen, not discoverable by our bodily senses, as
   being either past, future, or spiritual." It is trust "that Christ
   died for my sins, that he loved me, and gave himself for me."
3. Faith is the only necessary condition of justification.

These sermons by Wesley offer a substantial cross-section of the
basic points of his soteriology; however, the implicit doctrine of
justification by faith demands further dialectical clarification. As

William R. Cannon ably has shown,[24] Wesley's theology is based on this doctrine though not limited to it. And as we have contended in Chapter IV, this doctrine was central to the Aldersgate experience, even as it was fundamental to Wesley's entire theological reorientation, which began in that existential encounter with the Word.

Man responds to divine grace, Wesley held, on the condition of a God-given faith accompanied by repentance. The freedom implied makes possible the responsive and appropriating elements, though divine inspiration must be present. On condition of this faith, God justifies or accepts the sinner, who cannot merit the divine favor. This is the basic stage, as it were, of his salvation. Thus justification is strictly God's work, setting the individual in a new relation. Moralism or works righteousness cannot bring this about. Only grace, the divine love that is linked with divine judgment, while superseding it, can accomplish this. In itself the faith or degree of faith that this entails does not include good works so much as it inspires and leads to them on a new basis. Faith is a new disposition of the heart and is focused on the atoning and risen Christ meaningful here and now.

The grace that makes this new faith relation possible is looked upon by Wesley as universal, since extended to *all* men, but uniquely in the Gospel. As such it is neither limited to an elect number nor irresistible. It can be accepted or rejected as God has provided morally from within the grace-relationship. Though God is the source of justification, man is an important factor as he responds to the message and receives the Spirit of God's grace. The new relation thus gives man a new status in God's sight, while solely at God's bidding. Not a naturalistic experience, it is somewhat synergistic functionally, inasmuch as God and man work together. God gives and man receives, lest the revelation and redemption be incomplete.

Logically speaking, there is a sequence involved in justification, though it should not be dealt with explicitly in logical terms. Man is forgiven, acquitted, reconciled, adopted and regenerated.[25] Though one basic act, these facets of the matter suggest the primacy of the

---

24 William R. Cannon, *The Theology of John Wesley*, Chapters 4, 5, 6.
25 *Ibid.*, Chapter 6.

divine cause, while including the efficacy of it within man. Important is the new status given to sinful man, a reconciliation that opens up a genuine fellowship from the Godward side. In his *Notes on the New Testament,* Wesley writes concerning Romans 4:5 that Abraham was not justified by works but by faith alone. "Hence, we see plainly how groundless that opinion is, that holiness or sanctification is previous to our justification. For the sinner . . . has nothing to plead but his own guilt and the merits of a Mediator."[26]

Since the Holy Spirit is present, it can be said that justification is conditionally basic to regeneration and sanctification, the more elemental and more advanced aspects of the Spirit's work, respectively. Logically speaking, Calvinism places regeneration ahead of justification, implying the Spirit's work prior to the new status. There is no serious difference save that new birth *per se* is interpreted by Wesley more as the subjective effect than the objective cause. In either case, grace and the Spirit are essential and supersede anything man can do.

Justification by faith, it must be noted, was fundamental to Wesley's theology, yet he never reduced salvation theologically to Solifidianism. He thought that justification, though basic, was often abused by the Lutheran and Calvinist in whose hands it was "magnified to such an amazing size, that it quite hid all the rest of the commandments."[27] Wesley stood for a dynamic faith that was productive of good works in God's love, not merely a passive, unproductive faith. Repentance must accompany faith for it to be genuine. Says J. H. Overton of Wesley's view: "Justification implies only a *relative,* the new birth of a *real* change."[28] Or, perhaps better stated, justification is a relational change, the new birth an actuated change. God does something *for* him and *to* him when he justifies the believer, but also does something *in* him when he regenerates him. These are, however, merely aspects of the same initial Christ-experience, which removes the guilt and the power of sin, respectively. Justification restores man to the favor of God, but regeneration, holiness or sanctification, as we shall see, are what restores to him the image of God

---

26 Wesley, *Notes Upon the New Testament,* p. 371.
27 Wesley's *Journal,* Jan. 24, 1738, p. 419.
28 Overton, *op. cit.,* pp. 69–76.

in Christ, particularly the moral aspect of the image. Thus the sequel to justification as a new status is the work of the Spirit unto the new and mature life in the Spirit. It is to the doctrinal facets of this that we must turn in the next chapter.

CHAPTER VII

THE DOCTRINAL CONTENT
OF WESLEY'S THEOLOGY

(II)

THE WORK of the Holy Spirit is essential to every aspect of Christian salvation, as Wesley sees it. The Spirit not only accompanies the announced Word of deliverance to sinful men, but is basic to the divine work of reconciliation to which the gospel of Christ gives witness and summons. The doctrine of the Holy Spirit is indigenous, then, to Wesley's soteriology and applies especially to four major aspects of Christian salvation: regeneration, the witness of the Spirit, sanctification, and perfect love. A summary of each of these phases of salvation presupposes what has been discussed in the previous chapter, especially the meaning of justification as the groundwork of it all in the new relation established by God.

REGENERATION

Regeneration is the "new birth" of the believer in Christ and his work. It is what the Holy Spirit brings about in the sinner who is justified by faith. Thus what God basically does for a man is linked with what he does *to* and *in* a man. Though the entire work of the Holy Spirit may be broadly designated as sanctification ("making holy"), what is termed regeneration is elemental to it all, as Wesley views it. As the term "new birth" suggests, there is a fresh beginning and new-found vitality realized in the heart and life of the believer, as the Holy Spirit begins to redirect, remotivate and reenergize the justified man of faith. Thus the Holy Spirit is essential to the communion that arises between a man and God.

Justification, as we have seen above, makes for a new status, an

"adoption," as it were, which implies one's faith-conditioned acceptance by God.[1] Logically speaking, this precedes regeneration, according to Wesley, yet the work of the Spirit was involved in justification
also. The logical sequence, therefore, is not to be thought of as a
time sequence, as William R. Cannon has rightly emphasized,[2] lest
God be described as one who pardons a sinner while permitting him
to remain a sinner at the same time. Thus the Holy Spirit functions
any time the Gospel is efficacious in men's hearts, and this begins
with the repentant sinner who bows before God in faith.

Whereas justification is the new relation and new status before
God, regeneration is the acompanying new outlook, new ambition
and new disposition that comes to a man. It is because of this that
a person may experience the replacement of lower desires by new
and higher ones. Thomas Chalmers approached the meaning of this
in speaking of "the expulsive power of a new affection."[3] Thus regeneration is the Holy Spirit's work within the life of the man of
faith. This implies that the human spirit is now under the inspiration of the divine, making for new heart or a new motive and love
for the things of God. "A new heart will I put within thee," the Lord
promised men through the prophets Jeremiah and Ezekiel. This promise was a preview of the New Covenant in Christ, when a faith based
on a new faith-relation of love would supersede that based on law.

Regeneration has certain pronounced marks, Wesley indicated
in his preaching. Most pronounced is the Pauline trilogy of faith,
hope and love. Faith, then, is more than assent to sound doctrine.
Not only does it mean the condition by which a person is privileged
to be a child of God under grace, but subjectively it is "a disposition which God hath wrought in his heart."[4] This centers in the trust
that one is reconciled to God through the merits of Christ. This faith
also implies power over sin, with its "unholy desires and tempers,"
says Wesley. Accompanying such a faith is an inner peace, a serenity

---

[1] John Wesley, "The Spirit of Bondage and Adoption," in *Sermons on Several Occasions*, Vol. I (1794), pp. 170 ff.

[2] William R. Cannon, *The Theology of John Wesley*, Chapter 6.

[3] Thomas Chalmers, "The Expulsive Power of a New Affection," in *The
Greatest Sermons Ever Preached*, edited by Alexander Cairns.

[4] Wesley, "The Marks of the New Birth," in *Sermons on Several Occasions*,
Vol. I (1794), pp. 274 ff., 288.

of soul not known to the natural man. Also a present hope and as-surance of salvation, together with an impartial love for one's neigh-bors, including his enemies, and the ambition to obey God in all things and please his will out of a growing love for God in response to his love for us.

Regeneration may be thought of as the elemental work of the Spirit, the foundation, the threshold or basic phase of sanctification. Objective as He is, the Holy Spirit works subjectively in man that he may know the new birth and new heart within him. Regeneration, as Wesley saw it, includes the Holy Spirit's cleansing of the soul, an inner work of grace of which baptism is an outward sign. Not only is this forgiveness, but it is a renunciation of those sins that so easily beset us; hence a turning of one's back upon what has been our bondage. Thus not only does the Christian receive the imputed righteousness of the justified, but the infused grace to seek and fulfill a positive measure of what might be called an activated righteousness. That is, the Christian not only accepts his new standing before God, but gratefully and zealously seeks to live out that new standing, that he may lovingly reflect the nature and will of God in this life. Both experientially and doctrinally, justification is the threshold of sancti-fication, of which regeneration is the basic work of "first fruits of the Spirit." Just as regeneration makes for a new life of love, so it becomes a new life in power. The Spirit is both that love and that power, providing a positive victory over sin. Thus not only does God forgive the sinner, but enables him to avoid committing sin. The new relationship under grace is thereby efficacious in this life.

The regenerated man still finds life a struggle, but with a present hope both for this world and the next. Such a hope is relevant now and includes definite victories over sin. Two contrary forces are at work in the believer's life, the one being human nature's weaknesses or the "flesh," the other, grace or the Spirit.[5] Grace can surmount the flesh that gives occasion to sin. Not that God eradicates all evil tend-encies from man's fleshly nature, as Cannon has helped to clarify in behalf of Wesley,[6] but that God can enable a man to withstand

---

[5] John Wesley, "The Circumcision of the Heart," in *Sermons, ibid.,* pp. 259 ff.

[6] Cannon, *op. cit.*

temptation, even though sin is a perennial potentiality in his life. Though the carnal mind or nature is not destroyed or eradicated by regeneration, since its festerings are latent if not overtly active, it can be mastered. Wesley stressed this kind of victory with Johannine support.[7] Essential to the spiritual health that surmounts evil is a daily devotional communion with God, that the fruits of the Spirit may be borne fresh and live.

At times the regenerate person sins. This is due to his failure to rely upon the redemptive grace of God, his failure to allow the Spirit to possess his desires and affections as well as to empower his will to do God's bidding in all things. Such spiritual malnutrition, so to speak, leads to one's lower resistance; one's strength is weakened and one's love is diminished. Unless the believer repents and accepts both reinstatement and a replenishment of grace, evil is apt to continue to win out in concrete situations and true faith be lost. In some cases this leads to the so-called fall from grace that Wesley spoke of. The logic of this is that at all times the regenerate man is dependent upon the Spirit of grace both for his status and his power to obey God, to live righteously and reflect his love. Though free from the law of sin and death, he is not free from the law of holiness, the responsible side of his faith; rather, he freely accepts the law of holiness as an aspect of his faith and love for God and His Kingdom.

THE WITNESS OF THE SPIRIT

Wesley saw the faith that justifies to be the "evidence of things hoped for" (Hebrews 11:1). That is, when one has the faith, he knows it, and since the activity of God is behind that faith as a gift, the faith is in itself an important evidence of reconciliation. Where there is faith, Wesley maintained with the support of the apostle Paul, "the Spirit itself beareth witness with our spirit that we are the sons of God" (Romans 8:16; cf. I John 5:19). Accompanying the new birth, then, is a subjective assurance prompted by the objective witness of the Word and the Holy Spirit. Thus the man of faith is inspired to realize inwardly that he is in right relationship with

---

[7] Wesley, "The First Fruits of the Spirit," in *Sermons, op. cit.*, pp. 149 ff.

the Lord on the Lord's terms of grace. This is a part of being made a child of God, not merely by creation but by redemption. The outer witness is counterparted in the inner witness, and the soul "knows" he is reborn (I John).

In his sermon "The Witness of the Spirit,"[8] Wesley refers to a direct spiritual perception, an inner type of knowledge just as real as when the senses distinguish light from darkness. Included is a profound gratefulness to God.

Righteousness is imputed through grace and the merits of Christ, yet the imparted Spirit begins to bring to faith the virtues known as the "fruits of the Spirit." Wherever the Spirit functions, there are positive results or fruits. These include and add to the witness both inwardly and outwardly, as a passion for more of the blessings of the new life increases. Passion for the holy life is in itself an aspect of the witness. It belongs to "the love of God shed abroad in our hearts by the Holy Spirit."

The Wesleyan doctrine of personal assurance of salvation was something different from the Calvinistic idea of final perseverance or eternal security. It was assurance of a present pardon and justification. But both the assurance and status could be lost if the soul becomes careless about dependence on grace. Never soft-pedaling the doctrine of assurance, in his later ministry Wesley nevertheless claimed that the inner witness was not in itself a sure sign of one's salvation.[9] He saw how some enthusiasts might be too reliant on their feelings, placing them before the Word. In this respect, Wesley was both theologically sound and pastorally shrewd.

SANCTIFICATION

Sanctification is the basic work and increasing activity of the Holy Spirit begun in regeneration, when the justified soul became Spirit-endowed. As the term itself denotes, it means "being made holy" or the life process of holiness. This connotes not only an imputed righteousness, which *in itself* would remain antinomian if not

---

8 Wesley, *Sermons, op. cit.,* pp. 193 ff.

9 J. H. Overton, *John Wesley,* pp. 69 ff.

almost irresponsible, but also an imparted righteousness, an activated holiness. The new status of the justified believer has the goal of perfect love (I John 3:3, 4:17) and communion with the Father, an ongoing and growing experience under grace.

Sanctification also implies the cleansing of the soul, not only with forgiveness but a purging of the affections and desires unto victory over sin in this life. This means the Spirit can subdue the flesh; "the new creature in Christ" can overcome the "old man." Growth is realized in proportion to faith's reliance upon divine grace. Love *(agape)* qualifies and in large measure displaces self-interest *(eros)* as one moves from spiritual infancy to maturity. The ambition is to grow to the full stature of Christ and reflect God's love unto one's fellow men. Such a goal and height is called "Christian perfection." Somewhat frightening at first thought, it means that every capacity, motive, and ambition of one's life is Christ-centered. A life not simply anticipated, it can be realized now, Wesley held. Thus before God, in large measure, one is judged not 'only by what he claims by faith and hopes for, but *is*. Not an either/or, here is a dialectical both/and tension, which may be unacceptable to rationalistic theory but still feasible to the faith experience of Christian living.

All in all, faith is more than mere belief in any or all stages of Christian experience. Faith is a trustful commitment; hence, it is *belief with love*. Not merely an intellectual assent or grasp of doctrine, faith is the full moral and spiritual activity of one's whole, trusting self. To be saved in the maturest sense, there must be *"the faith which works by love* which, by means of the love of God and our neighbor, produces both inward and outward holiness." Holiness is the higher state of the saving relation, which while based on the grace of justification brings the righteous life to its positive fruition. Both justification and sanctification, then, are basic facets of a Christ-centered faith. Thus the main Wesleyan doctrines, soteriologically speaking, are repentance, justification by faith, and holiness of life. These may be likened to the porch, door, and abode of one's saving faith. Holiness then is synonymous with one's true love for God.

Sanctification is the Spirit's work, which restores the divine image in man, Wesley held.[10] Whereas justification is the passive aspect of salvation, sanctification is the more activated side. Thus salvation is not only *from* sin but to the *new* life of true freedom and lovingly accepted responsibility. Therefore, Wesley firmly states, "Beware of Antinomianism—'making void the law' or any part of it 'through faith.' Enthusiasm naturally leads to this; indeed they can scarce be separated." By law Wesley means the basic divine commandments, which not only define sins but guide· and direct the righteous life. By enthusiasm Wesley means "the imagining one has gifts of prophesying, or of discerning of spirits, judging people to be right or wrong by your own feelings."

Further elucidating the meaning of sanctification, Wesley admonishes:

> Beware of Solifidianism—crying nothing but Believe! and condemn-
> ing those as ignorant or legal who speak in a more scriptural way . . .
> in general our call is to declare the whole counsel of God, and to
> prophesy according to the analogy of faith. The written word treats
> of the whole and every particular branch of righteousness . . . "[11]

Not only did Wesley find it necessary to break with his Moravian friends over their emotional appeals, especially in the sentimental elements that cropped out in their hymns, but over their tendency to identify Christian devotion with mere belief, and in such a way as to feel little or no compunction to keep Christ's commandments. Similarly Wesley had to criticize Luther's tendency to depreciate the *positive* place for divine law in Christian life out of deference to the doctrine of justification. It is noteworthy that a century ago Sören Kierkegaard expressed in his *Journal* a similar criticism of Luther. Though Luther stressed the Decalogue, it was more to articulate sin than to articulate a holiness intrinsic to Christian faith and life in the Spirit. Wesley saw how this neglects much of the spirit of I John and the teachings of Our Lord. Grace frees men from sin and the law's condemnation but not from the law's moral demands. Good works done to attain salvation is sheer legalism; faith

---

10 *Ibid.*, pp. 80–84. Cf. pp. 69–76. For a thorough study of this doctrine, see Harald Lindström, *Wesley and Sanctification;* also W. E. Sangster, *The Path to Perfection.*

11 John Wesley, *A Plain Account of Christian Perfection,* pp. 139, 68–140.

without works is antinomianism; but faith with Spirit-prompted
works is the essence of holiness.

Considered to be one of the greatest of Wesley's sermons is
"The Original Nature, Properties and Use of the Law." This great
work truly reveals John Wesley to be a theologian. In it he traces
the moral law back to the mind of God as a part of God's nature.
Here he finds the basis for Christian ethics. The law convinces men
of sin and helps bring them unto Christ, then helps to keep them
spiritually alert. States Charles J. Little: "When I hear even Methodist preachers lauding the ethical superiority of modern preaching
I wonder from what materials they have framed their conception of
John Wesley."[12]

PERFECT 1)VE

The distinctive, though not exclusive, doctrine of Wesleyanism is
"Christian perfection." It has often been misinterpreted and distorted by many both outside and inside the Wesleyan camp. This
teaching does *not* imply freedom from ignorance, error, infirmities or
temptation, but it does imply freedom from volitional outward, or
actual, sin, evil thoughts and tempers. Wesley had the essentials of
this doctrine before 1738, but after that year it was given a sounder
footing in relation to justification, while it was made outstanding
throughout his most effective ministry as an appeal to mature Christian living.

Always the leader of the Evangelical Revival urged his followers
"to wait for entire sanctification" through obedience to God's com-
mands, denying themselves more in prayer and fasting. It was seldom to be attained in any other way. Yet holiness is not only joy,
but love of God and one's neighbor with all one's heart. Wesley never
professed to have reached that stage of holiness known as "perfect
love" or "Christian perfection," but he acknowledged those who
claimed they had.[13]

---

[12] Charles J. Little, *John Wesley, Preacher of Scriptural Christianity*, pp. 8,
118.

[13] Overton, *op. cit.*, pp. 80–84.

Before elaborating upon the doctrine of perfection or holiness, it would be well to consider further John Wesley's view of sin in the believer, for this is the problem addressed. In a sermon on this subject based on II Corinthians 5:17, Wesley refers to the ninth article of the Anglican Church. He states:

Original sin is the corruption of the nature of every man, whereby man is in his own nature inclined to evil, so that the flesh lusteth contrary to the spirit. And this infection of nature doth remain, yea in them that are regenerated; whereby the lust of the flesh . . . is not subject to the law of God. And although there is no condemnation for them that believe, yet this lust hath of itself the nature of sin.[14]

Wesley then refers to Galatians 5:17, saying, "The apostle here directly affirms that the flesh, evil nature, opposes the Spirit, even in believers that even in the regenerate there are two principles, contrary the one to the other." Wesley goes on further to say that the Corinthians to whom Paul wrote were Christians, but as "carnal" believers. He states: "Indeed this grand point, that there are two contrary principles in believers, nature and grace, the flesh and the Spirit, runs through all the epistles of St. Paul, yea, through all the Holy Scriptures. . . ." Wesley adds: "But can Christ be in the same heart where sin is? Undoubtedly, he can. Otherwise it never could be saved from sin. Where the sickness is, there is the physician,

Carrying on his work within,
Striving till he cast out sin."

Thus Christ is seen to dwell in the believer's heart who is really fighting against sin. Referring to the familiar verse in II Corinthians 5:17, Wesley says:

Now, certainly a man cannot be a new creature and an old creature at once. Yes, he may: he may be partly renewed, which was the very case with those at Corinth . . . the meaning of the words is this: His old judgment concerning justification, holiness, happiness, indeed concerning the things of God in general, is now passed away; so are his old desires, designs, affections, tempers, and conversation. All these are undeniably become new greatly changed from what they were. And yet though they are new, they are not wholly new. Still he feels,

[14] Wesley, *Works*, Vol. II, pp. 108 ff.

to his sorrow and shame, remains of the old man, too manifest taints
of his former tempers and affections, though they cannot gain any
advantage over him, as long as he watches unto prayer.[15]

Elaborating the doctrine of Christian perfection in the face of
the believer's problem of sin, we might note that Wesley revised and
enlarged the doctrine at different times, but it was always essentially
the same. The treatise in which he handles the doctrine most exhaus-
tively is *A Plain Account of Christian Perfection*. His purpose in this
work was to tell of the steps that led him to embrace the doctrine,
and why he thought of it as he did. In his early days the writings of
Bishop Jeremy Taylor, Thomas a Kempis, and William Law influenced him greatly in this respect, as suggested in Chapter IV. Their
works helped him to determine "to be all devoted to God—to give
him all my soul, my body, and my substance." In 1729, John Wesley
began to study the Bible as "the only standard of truth, and the
only model of pure religion." Thus he saw the need for the "mind of
Christ." Though this was before Aldersgate, let it not be overlooked
that Wesley never forsook the implications of the holy life he sought,
even though he failed to see the proper basis thereof until his Aldersgate experience. From then on, his life and theology were as diligent as ever but reoriented in the understanding of a justifying
grace.

In the *Plain Account* the main thoughts of Wesley's sermon
"The Circumcision of the Heart" are articulated as holiness. This
means not only forgiveness but being "cleansed" from sin of the
flesh and spirit, and in consequence endued with something of the
virtues of Christ, overcoming sin, and in Jesus' words, becoming,
"perfect even as your Father in heaven is perfect." Wesley explains
that perfection implies love. Of the believer's heart he says: "Let it be
continually offered up to God through Christ, in flames of holy love."
Everything done is in subordination to God's pleasure and will. In
his essay "The Character of a Methodist" (1739), Wesley asserts:

A Methodist is one who loves the Lord his God with all his heart,
with all his soul . . . mind, and . . . strength . . . He, therefore, is
happy in God; yea always happy, as having in him a well of water
springing up unto everlasting life, and overflowing his soul with

---

[15] *Ibid.*, pp. 108–12.

peace and joy. Perfect love having now cast out fear, he rejoices evermore . . . From him [God], therefore, he cheerfully receives all, saying, "Good is the will of the Lord"; and whether he giveth or taketh away, equally blessing the name of the Lord . . . He prays unceasingly, loves his neighbor . . . desires to do not his will but God's, keeps God's commandments, continually presents his body a living sacrifice, holy, acceptable to God, does all to the glory of God, doesn't lay up treasures upon earth, engages in no corrupt conversation . . .[16]

In another sermon Wesley treats the subject as follows:

I. *In what sense Christians are not perfect.*
   A. Limited respecting knowledge.
   B. Have weaknesses and slow understanding; temptations.
   C. "Impropriety of language."

II. *In what sense Christians are perfect.*
   A. Applying St. Paul's metaphor to St. John's assertion, Wesley says, "But even babes in Christ are so far perfect as not to *commit* sin [willfully]."
      1. John says, "He that is born of God sinneth not."
      2. "A just man falleth seven times (a day)"—this is "temporal affliction."
   B. "But it is only of grown Christians it can be affirmed they are in such a sense perfect as to be freed from evil thoughts and evil tempers." They are delivered from inward and outward sin. "He is purified from pride . . . from desire and self-will . . . anger . . ."[17]

This kind of righteousness, Wesley would have it understood, is to be experienced in this life in this world. As John says, "Herein is our love made perfect, that we may have boldness in the day of judgment, because, as he is, so are we in this world." It is a present, not future, action of cleansing—a *purification*, not merely a removal, of guilt. Wesley explains that John the Apostle speaks of two things, "to forgive us our sins" and then "to cleanse us from all unrighteousness." Here it is noteworthy that for Wesley sin exists in the justified person, while it is forgiven through Christ, whereas in the sanctified person sin is cleansed, that is, overcome by the Spirit, even subdued

[16] Wesley, *A Plain Account*, pp. 5–13, 15 ff.
[17] *Ibid.*, pp. 21–30.

sometimes to the point of nonexistence. The latter applies mainly to volitional sin, however, lest nothing be contested from the flesh (cf. I John 1:9, 2:1–28, 3:3–9, 22, 5:4).

Wesley asserts:

> This gift of God, the salvation of our souls, is no other than the image of God fresh stamped on our hearts . . . Not that they have already attained all that they shall attain, either are already in this sense perfect . . . They feel that all their sufficiency is of God, that it is he alone who "is in all their thoughts," and "worketh in them both to will and to do of his good pleasure" . . . Aforetime, when an evil thought came in, they looked up, and it vanished away. But now it does not come in, there being no room for this in a soul which is of God.[18]

One who trusts that his sins are forgiven is a child of God and an heir of His promises, but not all of salvation is fulfilled at once. An instantaneous work of the Spirit is followed usually by a gradual process of holiness. Says Wesley: "But we do not know a single instance, in any place, of a person's receiving, in one and the same moment, remission of sins, the abiding witness of the Spirit, and a new, a clean heart." Forgiveness and cleansing become two different aspects of salvation. When certain "bosom sins" are confessed and forgiven, the Spirit gives witness to the believer that he is a child of God. Sanctification is this due process of being renewed in the image of God, in righteousness and true holiness. The New Testament proffers men even further grounds for expecting to be saved from all sin as seen in the "prayers for sanctification." Examples are "Deliver us from evil" and Jesus' prayer in John 17, "Neither pray I for these alone, but for them also who shall believe on me through their word: that they all may be one, as thou, Father, art in me and I in thee, that they also may be one in us; I in them, and thou in me, that they may be made perfect in one." Wesley continues by calling to our attention the height of holiness as seen in Ephesians 3:14 ff., and I Thessalonians 5:23.

Both Charles and John Wesley maintained that, besides other aspects of Christian perfection set forth, "we are to expect it, not at death, but every moment, that now is the accepted time. . . ." The

---

18 *Ibid.*, p. 31.

Christian in this state is still dependent on Christ as set forth in the words "I am the vine . . ." Christ is the life and life giver. Both *voluntary* and *involuntary* sins need the atoning deed. The sanctified person can err or commit "involuntary sins," though Wesley does not call them sins. The term "sinless perfection," however, is *not* to be used, he points out, since it really contradicts itself.[19] "Perfect love" is the preferred term. In keeping with Wesley's view that it is possible to "fall from grace," he also believed it possible to lose Christian perfection.[20] Wesley once said that he had observed about five hundred people who knew perfect love, yet, while he sought it, he did not claim to have it himself.[21] Perfect love was equated with "full sanctification," "Christian liberty," and the *agape* of which Paul speaks in I Corinthians 13.[22] As a doctrine Wesley once spoke of it as "the grand depositum" of the Methodists.[23]

Answering certain questions Wesley gives us further insights into this challenging doctrine. He says that a person may judge himself to have attained holiness or perfection only—

When, after having been fully convinced of inbred sin, by a far deeper and clearer conviction than that he experienced before justification, and after having experienced a gradual mortification of it, he experiences a total death to sin, and an entire renewal in the love and image of God, so as to rejoice evermore, to pray without ceasing, and in everything to give thanks . . . None, therefore, ought to believe that the work is done, till there is added the testimony of the Spirit, witnessing his entire sanctification as clearly as his justification.[24]

This change can be experienced not through careless indifference, but only through the zealous keeping of God's commandments, and through earnest prayer and appropriate fasting. Men receive it by simple faith, but God gives that faith only when it is earnestly

---

19 *Ibid.*, pp. 34–67.
  20 John Wesley's letter to his brother Charles, circa 1762, *Letters of John Wesley*, edited by Eayers, p. 83.
21 Cf. Wesley's letter to the editor of *Lloyd's Evening Post*, London, March 5, 1767, in *Letters*, p. 122.
22 *Ibid.*, pp. 158, 372, 404.
23 Wesley's letter to Brackenburg, Bristol, Sept. 15, 1790, in *Letters*, p. 173.
24 Wesley, *A Plain Account*, pp. 68–140, 139.

sought. "Faith working or animated by love is all that God now requires of man." Fruits of this love are such as those Paul speaks of in Galatians. Those who are *perfect in love can grow* in grace, even to all eternity. Thus "perfect" is not a static term of love but a dynamic one. It bespeaks the motive more than the overt attainment. Love is the mark of a truly saved person as well as his goal. Love is the earnest that the Spirit is present; nothing can replace it.

Umphrey Lee critically summarizes Wesley's challenging and history-making doctrine in the following statement:

> What Wesley is talking about is, in brief, this. Man lives by faith, for faith is necessary if one is to have that love in the heart which is the cause of holiness. And holiness is necessary to final salvation, so necessary that, if man cannot have it otherwise, God will give it to him who has faith in the article of death. And in order to hold to this last, that man must be sanctified before he is finally saved even if on his deathbed, Wesley must hold that faith alone, without works, may be the condition of sanctification. So he goes on tortuously proving that, while works are in a sense necessary to sanctification, they are not necessary in the same degree as faith, not immediately and proximately.[25]

As readily seen, Wesley's doctrine of perfect love is as challenging as it may be frightening. It demands of the Christian that he live and die at his *best* in Christ, not at his least. Yet the common and realistic reaction might be: Who can attain unto such righteousness? But the scriptural demand carries with it a promise and hope and strength that belongs to the same grace that reinstates us. This is not to be minimized.

Two more basic criticisms arise, however. One is that Wesley, at times, spoke of grace or the Spirit as a quasi-metaphysical substance that enters the life of the believer and that needs restoration when lost or abused by one's negligence. This is to be questioned in view of what is primarily a relational view of salvation. The second criticism is that Wesley dealt with sanctification, at times, so as to imply literally that "without holiness no man shall see the Lord." This tends to undercut the significance or part of the significance of justification, since Wesley seems to suggest by this that no man could be acceptable to God in eternity until sanctified fully in this life. This

---

[25] Umphrey Lee, *John Wesley and Modern Religion*, p. 189.

tends to overlook what justification entails here. Furthermore, it may be expecting too much of finite men, some of them at least, even though under grace, for few shall attain unto perfect love. Yet it may be expecting the most of the Lord to see the possibility of such holiness, and this must not be scorned, overlooked or by-passed. The logic of this qualification is that Christians should leave the door open to perfect love rather than closed, for it remains a New Testament goal for the redeemed, whether they prove equal to it or not.

CONCLUSION

HAVING examined the main creative work and primary doctrines of John Wesley, one cannot fail to realize that this great evangelical preacher and church administrator possessed a truly creative and practical theology. Though in some respects rationally paradoxical, as in his bipolar dialectics, the system was experientially feasible. It greatly influenced people in recognizing the importance and vitality of Christian experience. Faith became potent and Christ vitally personal to the believer. Indeed Wesley's presentation of the Gospel made for a progressive Christianity, first, on the basis of a reappraisal of evangelical principles, and, second, on the basis of showing men the Gospel's existential relevance to their lives as individual persons.

The emphasis upon experience also met the demands of the scientific spirit of that age. Furthermore, a sovereign God became exceedingly personal through simple loving faith. Humanism could hardly stand up under such a theism. The emphasis upon the Spirit's witness made the God-man fellowship all the more vivid. The emphasis upon holiness prevented the development of an overly individualistic, though personal, salvation. It also demonstrated to others what Christ could do. The movement prevented eighteenth-century Christianity from becoming either spiritually sterile or socially stagnant in an age made increasingly complex by the social conditions that accompanied the Industrial Revolution.

In Chapter V it was stated that this theology was dialectically creative. This is true, we reiterate, for Wesley held to an Arminian freedom, yet a Reformed view of grace; justification by faith, yet holiness unto salvation; divine immanence, yet divine transcendence; human depravity, yet the imago dei's salvability; prevenient grace, yet fallen man; cleansed believers, yet sinning saints; voluntary sin, yet involuntary sin; a sovereign God, yet no closed election; biblical authority, yet experiential authority; substitutionary atonement, yet continuous atonement; the new creature in Christ, yet with taints of the old man; sin as a propensity, yet sin as a deed; witness of God's spirit, yet witness of our spirit; the objective Word, yet the subjective assurance; divine initiative, yet human choice; God-given faith, yet personal faith; prevenient grace, yet grace in faith and life.

Here there is a strong bifocal pattern of man before God. The views are both doctrinally defensible and scriptural. Do they not harmonize, after all, with the many unfathomably paradoxical elements in the New Testament drama of redemption, as chiefly portrayed in the very paradox of the Son of God Himself? Instead of being a stereotyped, thoroughly consistent, rational theology, does not this scheme, basically, leave more room for a dynamic "faith of the soul" made practical by experience? To be sure, Wesley's position is provocative, stimulating, and productive. Its re-evaluation today can add much to contemporary Protestantism, especially to challenge it to fulfill its total *possibilities* spiritually, ethically, and socially under God.

BASIC BIBLIOGRAPHY

Wesley, John. *The Journal of John Wesley*. Standard edition. Vol. I. London: Epworth Press, 1938.

———. *Letters of John Wesley*, Ed., George Eayres. New York: Hodder and Stoughton, 1915.

———. *Explanatory Notes Upon the New Testament*. 18th ed. New York: Eaton and Mains; Cincinnati: Jennings and Rye.

———. *Sermons on Several Occasions*. Vol. I. Philadelphia, 1794.

———. *Sermons on Several Occasions*. 2 vols. New York: Carlton and Phillips, 1853.

———. *The Standard Sermons of John Wesley*. Ed., E. H. Sugden, 2 vols. Lamar and Barton; Nashville: Publishing House, M. E. Church South.

———. *The Works of John Wesley*. *Sermons*. Vol. I, V, VI. London: Wesleyan Conference Office.

———. *Wesley's Works*. Vol I and II. New York: Methodist Book Concern.

———. *A Plain Account of Christian Perfection*. Nashville: Methodist Publishing House, 1855.

Anderson, William K. (ed.) *Methodism*. Nashville: Methodist Publishing House, 1947.

Benson, Louis F. *The English Hymn*. New York: Geo. H. Doran Co., 1915.

Bready, J. Wesley. *England Before and After Wesley*. New York: Harper Bros., 1938.

Cannon, William R. *The Theology of John Wesley*. Nashville: Abingdon Press, 1946.

Cell, George Croft. *The Rediscovery of John Wesley*. New York: Henry Holt & Co., 1935.

Douglas, Winfred. *Church Music in History and Practice*. New York: C. Scribner's Sons, 1937.

Ensley, Francis Gerald. *John Wesley, Evangelist*. Nashville: Tidings, 1955.

Gillman, Frederick John. *The Evolution of the English Hymn*. New York: Macmillan Co., 1927.

Hatfield, James Taft. *John Wesley's Translations of German Hymns*. Baltimore: Modern Language Association of America, 1896.

Herbert, Thomas W. *John Wesley as Editor and Author*. Princeton: Princeton University Press, 1940.

Hutchinson, Paul, and Luccock, Halford E. *The Story of Methodism*. New York: Methodist Book Concern, 1926; also the edition with Goodloe as co-author, New York: Abingdon Press, 1949.

Kennedy, Gerald. *Heritage and Destiny*. New York: Board of Missions, Methodist Church, 1953.

Lee, Umphrey. *John Wesley and Modern Religion*. Nashville: Cokesbury Press, 1936.

Lindstrom, Harald. *Wesley and Sanctification*. London: Epworth Press, 1950, 1956.

Little, Arthur W. *The Times and Teachings of John Wesley*. Milwaukee: Young Churchman Co., 1905.

Little, Charles J. *John Wesley, Preacher of Scriptural Christianity*. 1903.

MacArthur, Kathleen Walker. *The Economic Ethics of John Wesley*. New York: Abingdon Press, 1936.

McConnell, Francis J. *John Wesley*. New York: Abingdon Press, 1939.

McCutcheon, Robert G. *Our Hymnody*. New York: Abingdon-Cokesbury Press, 1937.

McDonald, W. *The Young People's Wesley*. New York: Eaton and Mains, 1901.

Methodist Hymnal, The. New York: Methodist Book Concern, 1935.

Overton, J. H. *John Wesley*. New York: Houghton, Mifflin and Co., 1891.

Piette, Maximin. *John Wesley in the Evolution of Protestantism*. Tr., J. B. Howard. New York: Sheed and Ward, 1937.

Pellowe, W. C. S. *John Wesley, Master in Religion*. Nashville: Parthenon Press, 1940.

Pike, G. Holden. *John Wesley and His Preachers*. London: Unwin, 1903.

Reeves, Jeremiah B. *The Hymn as Literature.* New York: Century Co., 1924.

Sangster, W. E. *The Path to Perfection.* London: Epworth Press, 1957.

Sherwin, Oscar. *John Wesley, Friend of the People.* New York: Twayne Publishers, 1961.

Stevens, Abel. *A Compendium History of American Methodism.* New York: Eaton and Mains, 1909.

Warner, W. J. *The Wesleyan Movement in the Industrial Revolution.* London: Longmans, Green and Co., 1930.

Williams, Colin. *Wesley's Theology Today.* New York: The Abingdon Press, 1960.

Wiseman, F. Luke. *Charles Wesley, Evangelist and Poet.* New York: The Abingdon Press, 1932.